Micropublishing

RECENT TITLES IN CONTRIBUTIONS IN LIBRARIANSHIP AND INFORMATION SCIENCE
SERIES EDITOR: PAUL WASSERMAN

Micropublishing

A
History of Scholarly
Micropublishing
in America,
1938–1980

ALAN MARSHALL MECKLER

Contributions
in Librarianship
and Information Science,
Number 40

GREENWOOD PRESS
WESTPORT, CONNECTICUT • LONDON, ENGLAND

Library of Congress Cataloging in Publication Data

Meckler, Alan M., 1945–
  Micropublishing: a history of scholarly micropublishing in America, 1938–1980.

  (Contributions in librarianship and information
science, ISSN 0084-9243; no. 40)
  Bibliography: p.
  Includes index.
  1. Micropublishing—United States—History. I. Title.
II. Series.
Z286.M5M4   070.5'795'0973   81-6955
ISBN 0-313-23096-X   (lib. bdg.)   AACR2

Library of Congress Catalog Card Number: 81-6955
ISBN: 0-313-23096-X
ISSN: 0084-9243

First published in 1982

Greenwood Press
A division of Congressional Information Service, Inc.
88 Post Road West
Westport, Connecticut 06881

Printed in the United States of America

10 9 8 7 6 5 4 3 2 1

To
Allen B. Veaner
a micropublishing pioneer

CONTENTS

ACKNOWLEDGMENTS

Many people have helped me in the preparation of this book. Allen B. Veaner, Director of the University of California Library (Santa Barbara) provided me with several of the ideas for the focus of the concluding chapter. Thanks also go to Paula Dranov who helped me check facts, and to John Walsh for his periodic readings of the manuscript.

I am also indebted to some of the micropublishing "pioneers" who took time from their schedules to meet with me. Vernon Tate, Eugene Power, Samuel Freedman, Alex Baptie, and the late Albert Boni were extremely kind in this regard.

Several people at Columbia University made a special effort to read the original manuscript. Thanks go to Hubbard Ballou and Margaret Steig of the Graduate Library School; to Stuart Bruchey, Henry Graff, and particularly James Shenton of the History Department; and to the late Louis Starr of the Department of Oral History.

Finally, I thank my wife Ellen and my children Naomi, Kate, Caroline, and John for their support and encouragement.

INTRODUCTION

For the past ten years scholarly micropublishing has been the focus of my career. I first became involved in this field while working for Greenwood Press, a Westport, Connecticut, publisher. My job was selling micropublications to libraries, and during a four-month period (November 1970 to February 1971) I contacted in person or by telephone nearly 300 college, university, and public librarians.

It soon became apparent to me that few, if any, of the librarians fully understood all the considerations involved in a decision to purchase a micropublication. While the content is usually obvious from the title ("United States Congressional Hearings" on microfiche needs no explanation) and certainly is the determining factor in terms of an individual library's need for a micropublication, librarians asked few questions about such basics as "finding aids," the keys to locating a specific document on microfiche or a reel of microfilm.

It is not difficult to understand the reason for their lack of familiarity with the factors that ultimately determine a micropublication's usefulness—its finding aids, the reduction ratio (for a definition, see the Glossary), and other aspects of technical quality. Few of the nation's graduate schools of library science offered courses in micrographics management. Furthermore, there was no independent source of information about scholarly micropublications. While new titles in every area of scholarship are reviewed, no such independent evaluation existed for micropublications.

In an attempt to meet what I saw as an important need, in March 1971 I founded the quarterly journal *Microform Review*. The first issue appeared in January 1972. It and each subsequent issue contains three to four articles on library micrographics management and fifteen to twenty microform reviews that analyze not only content but the technical quality of the publication as well, taking into consideration image quality and, if applicable, the accompanying finding aids.

Microform Review received an enthusiastic reception from the library community and, over the past seven years, has become acknowledged as the primary source for micropublication reviews. As its publisher, I have had a unique opportunity to observe and participate in the growth of scholarly micropublishing in the 1970s. I have often been asked about the history of micropublishing, and, despite the extent of my own involvement, I have had to confess ignorance of its origins and the pace of its growth prior to 1970.

My own curiosity about a field with which I have a daily concern, together with my educational background in history, seemed to dictate that I write a history of scholarly micropublishing in the United States. Certainly, the need for such a history is evident. Many articles have been written about specific events in the evolution of scholarly micropublishing, but neither a book-length approach nor a dissertation had been attempted. And, although the history of photography has been studied and written about in depth, only one book, Frederic Luther's *Microfilm: A History*, has documented the development of microphotography. It encompasses the period from the early nineteenth century to 1900. Any history of scholarly micropublishing, including this one, owes a debt to Luther's work.

In approaching my topic, it soon became evident that few primary sources were available for the study of microphotography and that I would therefore have to rely on some secondary sources and, to a large extent, on interviews. Surprisingly, few of the people interviewed had kept personal papers relating to their involvement with scholarly micropublishing. Several, particularly those entrepreneurs who entered the field solely as a commercial venture, simply did not bother to keep papers that might have had some historic value. Others lost or misplaced papers during the course of their careers, especially as businesses changed hands. Although some interviews took place by telephone or letters, most were conducted face to face in the United States, England, France, and Holland.

As this work progressed, two major themes emerged. The most obvious is the resistance to the use of micropublications among scholars. Although in the last forty years scholarly micropublishing unquestionably has greatly expanded the amount of available research materials, the fact remains that few people really like to use microforms. This resistance can be traced to two factors: a psychological one stemming from the inconvenience of placing a piece of machinery between the reader and the written word, and a related technological one stemming from the fact that the devices used to read microforms are largely unsatisfactory.

The second, overriding theme is the failure of micropublishing to fulfill the expectations of the pioneering scholars, librarians, scientists, and entrepreneurs who envisioned a future far more grandiose than today's modest realities. Microforms have not solved all the problems of libraries. They have not replaced the book as some predicted and others feared. They have improved, but have not revolutionized, libraries in two ways: (1) they help save space, and (2) they enable libraries to purchase publications that would be unavailable or prohibitively expensive in any other form.

If microphotography has revolutionized anything, it has been records-keeping in the business sector. Today, banks and other businesses, large and small, routinely store records ranging from canceled checks to invoices and purchase orders on microforms. In dollars and cents terms, the market for microforms and micrographics reading and copying equipment in business and industry surpasses that of scholarly micropublishing more than fivefold.

This study is by no means a technical analysis of micropublishing, although, of course, certain technological developments have determined the course of its history. (However, because some of the terminology may be unfamiliar to the reader, a glossary has been included and follows the Conclusions.) I have attempted to trace scholarly micropublishing as it evolved and expanded from its inception in the 1930s to the present. I have looked beyond its current status to consider the future in the light of past and present publishing economics. It is clear that in this age of spiraling inflation there will be increased demands on micropublishers to offer scholarly monographs, journals, and reference books that are too specialized to warrant the much greater costs of publication in hard copy. It is also evident that the expansion of research libraries will be determined, to a great extent, by what is both available and affordable and that scholarly micropublishing is uniquely suited to meet both those needs.

1

THE
EVOLUTION OF SCHOLARLY
MICROPHOTOGRAPHY

Scholarly micropublishing today owes its very existence to an evolutionary process dating back to the time of Alexander the Great: the development of photography and, subsequently, microphotography. This chapter reviews the history of photography and the refinements in the photographic process that made possible the reduction of a page of print to the minute image on today's microfiche.

Although the most significant photographic developments took place in the nineteenth and early twentieth centuries, the concept of photography is an ancient one. Aristotle described a rudimentary camera with a tiny opening or aperture that focused an image on a white screen in the back of the camera, a box large enough for an individual to enter and then trace the image on the screen.[1] By the mid-sixteenth century, lenses replaced the pinhole aperture, and the opaque screens gave way to translucent ones. Now, the image could be traced from outside the box, a technique that painters and others first adopted on a major scale.

Meanwhile, attempts continued to be made to capture the camera's image photographically. Although the alchemists of the "dark ages" knew that certain compounds of silver darkened under appropriate conditions, it was not until 1727 that a German chemist, Johan Schultze, proved that the mysterious darkening agent was, in fact, light. He placed black stencils over paper coated with silver chloride and created the first photograms, but he could not prevent the rest of the silver sheet from blackening as soon as the stencils were removed.[2]

In 1802, Thomas Wedgwood produced contact copies of leaves and painting on glass. Wedgwood, son of the well-known potter, claimed that his superposition printing was "useful for making delineations of all such objects as are possessed of a texture partly opaque and partly transparent."[3] This, however, was not photography: it merely depicted a visible image from a scene.

Seventeen years later, the English astronomer, Sir John Herschel, made a discovery that insured the success of modern photography. He found that a colorless salt compound (sodium thiosulfate) could dissolve the portion of the silver compound not previously exposed to light, leaving the exposed and blackened grains of silver unharmed.[4]

Herschel's work paved the way for the first photographs, but it was not until the 1950s, through the studies of Helmut and Alison Gersheim, that Joseph Nicephore Niepce finally was credited with producing the first photograph in 1826.[5] His effort was a poor specimen, both artistically and technically.[6] Niepce's partner, Jacques Mande Daguerre, had more luck, and history records that he took the first successful photograph. In 1839, Daguerre developed a process whereby a photograph could be produced on a silver-coated copper plate treated with iodine. This "Daguerreotype" produced fine pictures of inanimate objects; improvements in the speed of the plate soon made it appropriate for portraits as well.

That same year, an Englishman, William Henry Fox-Talbot, devised an alternative process, a negative-positive technique (calotype) in which sensitized paper was used instead of metal plates. Although Talbot's photos lacked the fine detail of Daguerre's, they were easier and cheaper to produce, and the process itself allowed for duplicate prints.[7]

Still another photographic breakthrough occurred in 1839—the production of a microphotograph by John Benjamin Dancer, the son of a Liverpool, England, microscope and optical manufacturer, Josiah Dancer. Dancer's interest in photography was stimulated by the news of Daguerre's and Fox-Talbot's discoveries. Dancer began to experiment and within several weeks had produced satisfactory pictures with the Daguerreotype process. Then, combining the Daguerreotype process with a microscope, he installed a microscope lens (of 1½ inch focal length) in a camera and produced a microphotograph. His subject was a document measuring 20 inches long. With a 160:1 reduction, the image was ⅛ inch long, but the writing was legible under a 100× microscope.[8]

Although Dancer continued to make microphotographs using the Daguerreotype process, he considered them novelties. It was left to his son to describe the microfilm camera and operating method Dancer developed:

> An ordinary microscope was not used. A bat's wing burner furnished the light (behind a conventional large-size negative) and this was placed inside an optical lantern, the image passing through a lens and condensing system giving a convergent beam of light, the latter finally entering the microobjective (in the case a ½″) from the back. The whole thing was horizontal, and the entire apparatus was enclosed in a canvas-covered tent, a sort of improvised dark room.[9]

In 1851, twelve years after Dancer produced the first microphotograph, development of another technique—the wet collodian process—furthered the evolution of photography and microphotography. Developed by Frederick Scott Archer, this new process utilized cellulose nitrate (guncotton) dissolved in ether and alcohol. A glass plate was coated with the solution and then sensitized by immersion in a bath of silver nitrate.[10]

Others experimenting with microphotography at the time included George Shadbolt, editor of *The Photographic Journal,* who for many years claimed microphotography as his own invention but finally recanted.[11] A. Rosling, treasurer of the Photographic Society of London, exhibited the first newspaper microphotographs in pages from the *Illustrated London News* and described them as follows:

> In every instance I have found the definition perfect; and the one now on the table is the eight-hundredth part of the original size; the length of the lines composing the lens is the seven-hundred-and fiftieth part of an inch, and about half the thickness of the human hair.[12]

The work of Dancer, Shadbolt, and Rosling inspired a glowing tribute from the editors of the eighth edition of the *Encyclopaedia Britannica,* published in October 1857:

> Among the wonders of microscopic photography not the least interesting and useful are the fine microscopic portraits taken by Mr. Dancer of Manchester, and copies of monumental inscriptions so minute, that the figures in the one, and the letters in the other, are invisible to the eye. A family group of seven complete portraits occupies a space the size of the head of a pin; so that the *ten thousand* single portraits could be included in a square inch.

> Microscopic copies of dispatches and valuable papers and plans might be transmitted by post, and secrets might be placed in spaces not larger than a full stop or a small blot of ink.[13]

Yet, not everyone appreciated microphotography. Thomas Sutton's *Dictionary of Photography* published in 1858 dismissed it as "childish" and "useless."[14]

Although Dancer was the inventor of microphotography, he was not the first to suggest using it for scholarly purposes. Until recently, it was believed that the idea first was proposed by Sir John Herschel in the early 1850s, but research now indicates that it was made almost simultaneously by James Glaisher, an English astronomer. In 1851, Glaisher attended the Great Exhibition in London and was appointed reporter for the class (number X) entitled "Philosophical Instruments and Processes Depending on Their Use." In the introduction to his report, Glaisher devoted two of the three pages to "the most remarkable discovery of modern times—the art of Photography." He went on to argue for the use of microphotography in the preservation of documents.[15]

Herschel also attended Class X, and two years later in a letter to his brother-in-law, John Stewart, he made his first written suggestion for microphotographing documents. Then, on July 6, 1853, Herschel wrote to the editor of the *Athenaeum:*

Your insertion of the annexed letter from my brother-in-law Mr. John Stewart, of Pau, will much oblige me. The utility of this mode of reproduction seems indisputable. In reference to its concluding paragraph, I will only add, that the publication of concentrated microscopic editions of works of reference—maps, atlases, logarithmic tables, or the concentration for pocket use of private notes and MSS, &c., &c. and innumerable other similar applications—is brought within the reach of any one who possesses a small achromatic object-glass of an inch and a half in diameter.[16]

In a letter to Herschel, Stewart, after describing the difficulties of producing the original master copy of a microphotograph, explained: "Thus, by the simultaneous action, if necessary, of some hundreds of negatives, many thousand impressions of the same picture may be produced in the course of a day." And he concluded: "Should your old idea of preserving public records in a concentrated form on microscopic negatives ever be adopted, the immediate positive reproduction on an enlarged readable scale, without the possibility of injury to the plate, will be of service."[17]

Not long afterward, in 1858, Rene Patrice Dagron, a Frenchman, patented the first microfilm viewer. Although his skill as a microphotographer of novelty items brought him great wealth, Dagron is best remembered for the idea of having pigeons carry messages on microfilm to the besieged city of Paris in 1870. Each film weighed one-twentieth of a gram, and each pigeon was able to carry several hundred messages; a total of 60,000 to 80,000 messages were delivered.[18]

Despite the work of Dancer, Dagron, Herschel, and Glaisher, microphotography was not regarded as a significant achievement. To establish microfilm and microphotography as acceptable tools, it would take more technological advances, plus industry's recognition of their space-saving qualities. However, developments in the field continued on both sides of the Atlantic. In the United States, the Lanheim brothers produced the first microphotographs mounted on microscope slides in the 1850s,

and in 1863 the American Photographic Society announced that
one of its members, Colonel Nicholas Pike, had successfully
produced microscopic pictures using methods similar to
Dagron's.[19]

The first establishment in the United States devoted to producing microfilm novelties was John H. Morrow's studio at 14 John
Street in New York City. Morrow, who had corresponded with
both Dancer in Manchester and Dagron in Paris, also offered a
course for prospective microfilm technicians.[20] His studio and
microfilm business were enthusiastically described by a New
York newspaper reporter:

> Mr. Morrow has opened his rooms and is prepared to do
> any amount of work, which, from a number of specimens
> we have seen, is most excellent and charming. We were
> shown opera-glasses, watch charms, finger-rings, breast-
> pins, eye-glasses, knives, canes, penholders, pencils, pipes,
> portemonnaies, &c. in great variety. By close examination,
> a little sparkling dot would be found, not as large as the
> head of a pin. Looking through these, we would see the
> most wonderful beauties, such as masonic certifications,
> portraits of fifty people, all distinct, or it might be the Cabi-
> net, our own picture, or that of some other distinguished
> individual. . . . Mr. Morrow took great pains to show us his
> whole operandi of printing &c., which was very novel and
> interesting.[21]

Dancer and Dagron popularized the use of microfilm on a
transparent base; the original Daguerreotype reductions had
been produced on opaque-base substances. Transparent bases
allowed for greater ranges of contrast and higher degrees of
resolution between closely spaced microscopic lines. Most of the
microfilm produced since Dancer's time has been on transparent
bases. (Later chapters of this book discuss the microprint and
microcard, which were developed in the twentieth century, and
which are opaque-based microreproductions.)

In 1870, George Scamoni, a photographer for the Russian
Imperial Office in Saint Petersburg, devised one of the first

workable methods of producing microprints. His *Handbuch der Heliographie* explained that the process relied upon building a silver matrix in exaggerated relief from a positive collodian print. By copper-coating the matrix via electrolysis, Scamoni obtained a relief printing plate in metal.[22] He adapted this method to small-size photocopies and succeeded in reproducing a page from a German illustrated magazine, *Uber Land und Meer.* Scamoni advocated using his process to conceal maps in military operations.[23] Nevertheless, microphotography was still regarded as a novelty rather than as useful technology. What is more, there were practical obstacles to its use. First, the process was unfamiliar both to industry and the public; second, no standardized cameras and viewers were available. (In fact, no company manufactured the equipment at this time.)

It was not until the 1920s that micrographics equipment was produced in any quantity, although a variety of developments continued to improve the technology. In 1879, Thomas Arthur Dillon received a patent for a semi-automatic camera capable of filming twenty documents consecutively before reloading was necessary. And in 1880, George Eastman founded the Eastman Dry Plate Company. Eight years later, he introduced the Number 1 Kodak which, with its slogan, "You push the button—we do the rest," brought photography to the amateur. It also provided a basic lens adaptable for textual reproduction. In 1889, the standardization by Thomas A. Edison "on film 35 mm (1⅜ inches wide) in long ribbon form for motion picture use set the pattern for development of compact, high quality cameras for microfilming."[24] Then, in 1890, Soren C. Madsen of Sleepy Lake, Minnesota, applied for a patent on a "multiplying-back dry plate camera" used for producing frames the size of a postage stamp.

Finally, in 1896, microphotography's potential was recognized through the work of Reginald A. Fessenden, a Canadian radio engineer. Fessenden conceived of a photographic process whereby he could copy 2,000 words a minute. He was motivated by the realization that "the engineer sooner or later comes to the point where he can no longer rely upon his memory for the col-

lection and preservation of his technical and scientific data.''
The technical significance of Fessenden's contribution is overshadowed by his speculations about the potential of microphotography:

> The success of this method has caused the writer to indulge
> in some speculation as to the possibility of an extended use
> of the photographic method for publishing books. The
> smallest writing of which the writer is aware is that men-
> tioned by Morton, *Cassier's Magazine,* August, 1895. This
> specimen referred to is so small that 6,000,000 words of
> similar size would go within the space of one square inch.
> A little calculation shows that letters one-fifth the size
> could be plainly read with a microscope of the highest pos-
> sible power, so that the theoretical limit would be
> 150,000,000 words per square inch.
>
> Even with a magnification of 30 diameters, instead of the
> 600 which I have assumed in the previous calculations, one
> such volume would go on a plate one inch square. At this
> rate a box one foot cube would contain a library of 50,000
> volumes, or 1,500,000 with the larger magnification. How-
> ever startling this may seem, it is not impractical at least for
> the lower power mentioned, and it is well within the bounds
> of possibility that the scientific student of the future will do
> his book work with the aid of a small projection lantern
> and a library of small positives, purchased at a small frac-
> tion of the price now paid.[25]

At the same time, the library world was recognizing the need
for a reliable photoduplication process. The Eastman Kodak
Company offered the Photostat, the trade name for a subsidiary
of Eastman Kodak. While it was not the first of its kind, the photostat soon became commonplace in institutions that could afford
it.[26] Basically, it was an oversize bellows camera that took a picture on a roll of sensitized paper rather than on transparent film.
By 1912, the Library of Congress in Washington, D.C., the John
Crerar Library in Chicago, and the New York Public Library in

New York City had installed photostat cameras. As these machines proliferated, the idea of reproducing photographically rare and inaccessible originals began to gain acceptance among scholars and librarians.

Meanwhile, a variety of events were combining to further the development of microphotography. In 1900, George Biedler of Oklahoma City invented a photocopy machine and in 1904 organized the Rectigraph Company. Eventually, Rectigraph became part of the Haloid Company, which subsequently changed its name to the Xerox Corporation. And in Belgium in 1906 the archivist-engineer team of Paul Otlet and Robert Goldschmidt advanced the first significant proposal for the modern microfiche. Otlet, a librarian, was fired by a dream of creating a World Center Library of Juridical, Social, and Cultural Documentation, but he realized that it was both impractical and unwieldy to bring together all the books such a center would demand. To solve the problem of space he turned to Goldschmidt, an engineer, and together they conceived of a new form of publication—the form we now know as the microfiche.

Otlet and Goldschmidt first presented their ideas at a conference of the International Federation of Documentation in 1906 in Marseilles, France. In their paper, entitled *Sur une forme novelle du livre: le livre microphotographique* [On a New Form of the Book: The Microphotographic Book], they envisioned a microphotographic book that differs from today's microfiche only in size and matrix. They suggested a format of 75 mm × 125 mm (the international standard size of a library catalog card), with seventy-two pages arranged in six rows of twelve columns wide. (The most widely used microfiche today measures 105 mm × 148 mm and contains ninety-eight pages arranged in seven rows of fourteen columns.)

After describing the inadequacies of book distribution, costs, and space considerations, Otlet and Goldschmidt presented their arguments for the new form of the book:

> . . . one can deduce, as desiderata, that there is a place for a new form of book that avoids the inconveniences pointed out and will produce works in the future: (1) of lightweight

and reduced size, (2) of uniform dimensions, (3) of un-
changeable substance, (4) of moderate price, (5) easy to pre-
sever, (6) easy to use, and (7) available for continual reproduction, i.e., copies or duplicates can be made on demand.

As to the problem of reading the microfiche, they offered the
following suggestions:

The second problem to consider is the utilization of the
microphotographic document, that is, enlargement for
reading.

In order to be practical, this enlargement has to be done in-
stantaneously, by compact devices of smallest dimensions
and whose use will not fatigue the viewer.

. . . Luminous projection is currently in use. In the labora-
tories and the lecture halls, not only ordinary views are
projected, but also microscopic negatives.

If one places the film negative described earlier in a very
simple enlarger, lit by an electric lamp and provided with a
magnifying glass, the image may be increased according to
the variable dimensions which can be projected on a
ground glass that closes the opposite side of the *camera
obscura*. It is there that the reading of the text will take
place. A slide positioned on the stage of a microscope of the
carriage of a typewriter, will circulate the fiche from left to
right and top to bottom. Then at the reader's will, the
microphotographic pages on each centimeter of the film
will come successively in front of the lens to be read.

Their proposal concluded with a plea that their ideas be given
serious consideration, and not be dismissed as science fiction or
wishful thinking.

It is natural that such results appear as miraculous, and at
first glance one's mind renounces such goals and deems
them impossible. But do we not live in an age where according to a repeated formula, the utopia of yesterday is the
dream of today, the reality of tomorrow?

To build the most serious hopes, we will recall simply the following result, already achieved and largely applied, of the combination of micrographics and of enlargement by projection. In a small metal box 15 centimeters in diameter and 2.5 centimeters deep, we can now store a roll of motion picture film 50 meters long. The roll reproduces 5,000 scenes. Each of these can be projected on a canvas capable of covering 16 square meters. The small box therefore contains within it, so to speak, a minuscule volume, the material necessary to project at will and repeatedly 80,000 square meters of photographic documents![27]

Their hopes, however, were not realized. The Federation did ask them to continue their work, and Goldschmidt did design a reading device for a microfiche, but neither it nor the microfiche received support. By 1911, Otlet and Goldschmidt had abandoned their project.

Despite this setback, other developments were furthering the cause of microphotography. In the United States, the American Telephone and Telegraph Company advanced the idea of offering telephone directories on microfilm.[28] And in 1906 Otto Vollbehr of Berlin announced the development of his microphotoscope, a small hand viewer that could be used in the dark with an illuminating box.

In 1908, Amandus Johnson designed his own microfilm camera for bibliographical microfilming.[29] As a researcher, Johnson had copied many manuscripts, a laborious process that presented problems of errors and illegibility. He determined that the best means to insure accuracy was copying by photography. Using first an unwieldy 5 × 7 inch plated camera together with glass plates and holders and later a more compact German camera, Johnson managed to copy his manuscripts photographically.

It was at a Philadelphia movie theatre that Johnson hit upon his radically new approach to photographing documents.

As I entered (the theatre), the text of a letter was projected on the screen. It was perfectly readable. This gave me an idea. When the showing was over, I asked the manager for permission to visit the projection room. . . . I was now con-

vinced that the most efficient and practical manner to photograph manuscripts was by a strip of continuous film on a
roller and placed in a camera that would be operated by a
crank to move the film in taking the pictures.

He went on to describe the construction of the first 35 mm
microfilm camera:

> As mechanics and carpentry are my two hobbies, I had no
> difficulty in making a model of such a camera. I cut two
> small wooden centers from a broom handle, to each of
> which I attached two circular cardboard discs four inches
> in diameter . . . thus making two spools that would take
> 100 feet of film each. The side of the camera could be opened
> for loading; below I attached my miniature camera.

Johnson then modestly assessed his contribution to microphotography: "By proving to many . . . that microfilming could be
done to great advantage at small cost, I may have made a contribution to microfilming by giving it a start earlier than otherwise
would have been the case."[30] These mechanical developments,
plus the work of Otlet, Goldschmidt, Fessenden, and Johnson,
provided nearly all the ingredients for the practical implementa-
tion of microphotography, but it still lacked widespread acceptance.

In 1925, Otlet and Goldschmidt teamed up again to explore the
possibilities of micropublishing. This time they prepared a paper
entitled "The Microphotographical Book: A Communication on
the Subject of Recent Technical Work on New Forms of Books
and Documents: Practical Results and Organizations." They
envisioned a library of the future where

> practically speaking, one can preserve in a Central Agency
> a negative and positive of each volume or each series of
> documents, each film being capable of being used to make
> an unlimited number of copies.

In this same Center the positive copies will be provided for use with reading machines made available for loan or put on sale. The reproductions, in format, number and on a requested material-film or sensitized paper, will be transmitted on request to those who are interested. A very simple method will permit one to retrieve rapidly the desired film and that part of it which is of interest. One might thus so easily complete the documentation which is currently limited to giving the titles of works, by providing instead the texts themselves.[31]

Despite their far-sighted proposals, the catalyst for microphotography's eventual hard-won acceptance was the Check-O-Graph microfilm camera, the invention of George L. McCarthy, a one-time bank manager. At the age of thirty-nine, McCarthy had become vice-president of the Empire Trust Company of New York. Like Amandus Johnson, he was fascinated with moving pictures and envisioned "documents traveling on a series of endless belts" that could be filmed at high speed."[32] Being neither an engineer nor a scientist, McCarthy had no preconceived notions of how to go about producing his camera. He tried something new:

Having dismissed the conventional between-the-lens and focal plane shutters of the still cameras, and the butterfly shutters of the movie camera, he decided to sack the shutter completely. Instead, the film and the copy would pass on either side of the open lens in perfect synchronization. The image on the film would consequently be "frozen" as both the document and the film were traveling at the same relative speed.[33]

It worked, and by 1926, McCarthy had produced ten of his Check-O-Graphs. He then entered into an agreement with the Kodak Company. McCarthy became general manager of what became known as the Recordak subsidiary of Kodak, and Kodak undertook to manufacture and sell his camera.[34]

After some improvements by Kodak, the first Check-O-Graph was installed at McCarthy's old bank on May 1, 1928. Other banks soon adopted the system, and the microfilm industry was born. Banks could now dispense with handwritten transcripts of foreign checks; book-keeping departments were protected from depositors who might claim improper charges had been made on their accounts; and depositors could prove a payment had been made even if a canceled check had been misplaced.[35]

Kodak was followed into micrographics by the Remington Rand Corporation, which in 1929 acquired the rights to a micro-film camera invented by R. M. Hessert that photographed both sides of documents. As with the Check-O-Graph, the first users of this new equipment were banks and other commercial establishments. Commercial microfilming was, at last, a reality. Other applications including scholarly uses would soon follow.

NOTES

1. Frederic Luther, *Microfilm: A History, 1839–1900* (Silver Spring, Md.: National Microfilm Association, 1965), p. 8.

2. Ibid., p. 9, and Hubbard W. Ballou, "Photography and the Library," *Library Trends* 5 (1956): 265.

3. Helmut and Alison Gersheim, *The History of Photography* (New York: Oxford University Press, 1955), p. 32.

4. Luther, *Microfilm*, p. 9.

5. Ibid., p. 10.

6. Gersheim, *History of Photography*, p. 39.

7. Luther, *Microfilm*, p. 10, and Ballou, "Photography and the Library," p. 266.

8. Joseph Sidebotham, "On Micro-Photography," *Photographic Journal* 6 (1857): 91. It should be noted that William Henry Fox-Talbot made reduced-size photocopies of a deed to land ownership prior to 1846. The letter is reproduced in Nicolas Barker's *Portrait of an Obsession: The Life of Sir Thomas Phillipps, the World's Greatest Book Collector* (New York: G. P. Putnam, 1967), p. 138.

9. John Benjamin Dancer Papers, University of Texas Library, Austin, Tex. Additional information on Dancer can be found in the Archive of Micrographics, Annapolis, Md.

10. Gersheim, *History of Photography*, p. 151, and G.W.W. Stevens, *Microphotography* (New York: John Wiley & Sons, 1968), p. 3.

11. Luther, *Microfilm*, p. 21, and L. L. Ardern, *John Benjamin Dancer* (London: The Library Association, 1960), pp. 1–19. Although there was general knowledge of Dancer's work in the scientific community, the fact that he was producing microphotographs as early as 1852 was not well known outside of Manchester.

12. Minutes of the second ordinary meeting, *Journal, Royal Photographic Society* 1 and no. 2 (1859).

13. *Encyclopaedia Britannica*, 8th ed., "Microscope."

14. Thomas Sutton, "Microphotography," in *Studies in Micropublishing*, Allen B. Veaner, ed. (Westport, Conn.: Microform Review, Inc., 1977), p. 88.

15. *Exhibition of the Works of Industry of All Nations 1851. Reports by the Juries on the Subject in the Thirty Classes into which the Exhibition was Divided* (London, 1852), p. 243.

16. *Athenaeum*, no. 1341 (1853): 831.

17. Ibid.

18. Dagron's complete report on the service can be found in *La Poste par Pigeons Voyageurs* (Tours: Typographie Lahure, 1871), pp. 1–24.

19. Nicholas Pike, "The Micrograph," *Photographic Notes* 9 (1864): 21.

20. Luther, *Microfilm*, p. 43.

21. Ibid.

22. Ibid.

23. Ibid.

24. Ibid., p. 96, and the Archive of Micrographics file on the Eastman Kodak Company.

25. Reginald A. Fessenden, "Use of Photography in Data Collections," *Electrical World* 28 (August 22, 1896): 224.

26. Vernon D. Tate, "Reflex and Photocopying," in *The Complete Photographer* (New York: National Education Alliance, 1942), pp. 3086–99.

27. Robert Goldschmidt and Paul Otlet, *Sur une Forme Nouvelle du Livre: Le Livre Microphotographique* (Brussels: Institut International de Bibliographie, 1906), pp. 1–12. (This article originally appeared in French. This translation appears in *Studies in Micropublishing*, Veaner, ed.)

28. Ian Montagnes, "Microfiche and the Scholarly Publisher," *Scholarly Publishing* 5 (1975): 132.

29. Amandus Johnson, "Some Early Experiences in Microphotography," *Journal of Documentary Reproduction* 1 (1938): 9–19.

30. Quoted in James Mann, *Reducing Made Easy* (Durham, N.C. Moore Publishing Co., 1976), pp. 33–34.

31. Robert Goldschmidt and Paul Otlet, "The International Preservation and Propagation of Ideas," in *Studies in Micropublishing,* Veaner,
ed., pp. 109–16.

32. Mann, *Reducing Made Easy,* p. 34.

33. Ibid.

34. Ibid.

35. Ibid., p. 36, and the Archive of Micrographics file on the Eastman
Kodak Company.

2

THE EARLY YEARS

Although the technology for scholarly micropublishing was available as early as 1928, publishers, scholars, and librarians remained either unaware or unconvinced of its value as a research tool. In order to remedy this situation, two prestigious groups, the Social Science Research Council (SSRC) and the American Council of Learned Societies (ACLS) established a Joint Committee on Materials Research.

The SSRC had been organized in 1933 at the instigation of the American Political Science Association's committee of research headed by Charles E. Merriam of the University of Chicago.[1] Its purpose was to advance the social sciences. The ACLS was established in 1919 as a private representative of the humanities in the scholarly world.[2] These two groups gathered in August 1929 in Hanover, New Hampshire, to found the Joint Committee on Materials for Research. They acted in response to increasing requests from scholars for greater access to European archives, especially through microphotography. By this time, librarians, too, had recognized the value of preserving crumbling editions of newspapers and other printed materials on microfilm.[3]

The SSRC and ACLS set forth as one of the new committee's goals the improvement and preservation of a constantly expanding body of research materials vital to scientific progress in several fields.[4] Accordingly, the committee settled upon seven courses of action to meet its objectives, two of which were of particular importance to scholarly micropublishing:

Initiating and participating in plans to discover, select, edit, publish or otherwise reproduce basic data in the social sciences which are difficult of access to students or likely to perish.

Calling to the attention of individuals and of governmental, business, and other institutions and agencies the importance of preserving their records for future analysis and study.[5]

The work of the joint committee was directed by Dr. Robert C. Binkley[6] who had become interested in scholarly resource development while pursuing his doctorate in history at Stanford University. While writing his dissertation, Binkley served as reference librarian (1923–1927) at the Hoover War Library and was responsible for classifying the confidential materials in the vault of the library. This task triggered his interest in using microfilm to resolve the problems of space and paper deterioration inherent in the preservation of research materials.[7]

The results of the joint committee's work were presented in a 1931 report, *Methods of Reproducing Research Materials: A Survey Made for the Joint Committee on Materials for Research of the Social Science Research Council and the American Council of Learned Societies,* which reviewed in exhaustive detail publishing and library costs, as well as the various methods then available for reproducing research materials. It found two formats suitable to the reduction of text to minute proportions on photographic film or plate.[8] The first was the photostat, and the second was what Binkley described as "a device which is independent of book manufacturing and which will put before the scholars' eyes an image of a text projected on a screen, rather than the tangible page of a book."[9] This alternative, which Binkley referred to as "filmslides" (today, we would call it "microfilm"), promised in his estimation "the most sweeping changes in the cost level at which research material can be produced."[10]

Addressing a particular area of concern to the joint committee, the reduction ratios of original materials, Binkley argued that "as the processes verge from the typographic toward the photographic, the size of the edition becomes less significant as a controlling element in costs, and the size of the letters becomes more important."[11] Using 1931 prices, he provided a dramatic example of what he meant, explaining that

> a fifty page issue of *The New York Times* covers with print two hundred and seventy square feet of paper surface. It sells for three cents on the street. Photographed full size it will cover eighty-six dollars worth of photostat paper; reduced twenty-three diameters it will fit on three cents worth of film.[12]

At the same time, other methods of reproducing scholarly materials were being advanced. The photoscope was introduced in the late 1920s and early 1930s, and a Belgian company marketed *Films "microphote" de la Phtocopie* as a "cheap but efficient substitute for glass slides used in art study and visual education."[13] The libraries of historical associations in Europe were encouraged to adopt the photoscope to preserve historical materials, but as it was suitable only for illustrative materials for lectures, it fell into disuse after the mid-1930s.

In the late 1920s and early 1930s, companies like Ansco, Leica, and Lemare designed and manufactured cameras for filming industrial or commercial products. However, the most suitable machine for research purposes was the Filmograph. It could take 400-foot rolls of film, and it functioned as follows:

> A volume of records is placed in a glass-covered holder; the attendant presses down the glass cover which releases the camera shutter. An electric motor opens the shutter for the exact exposure time required. When the exposure has been made a bell rings, which notifies the attendant that he may raise the glass, turn the page, and press down the cover again.[14]

Commercial publishers had begun to take some interest in micropublication of scholarly materials, as evidenced by this suggestion from the Filmograph Library Service to Robert Binkley:

... a plan in contemplation whereby the persons interested will make available to persons and institutions desiring such service, what will probably be known as a Filmograph Library Service. The purpose of this service will be
to make available Filmograph duplicates of invaluable
manuscripts in this and other countries which would not
otherwise be available to persons and institutions at a distance from the original material.

These Filmographs with explanatory notes by noted
authorities and custodians would be classified into various
types of Filmograph Libraries to be rented or sold to those
desiring them. . . . Many variations of the plan might be
developed including the interchange of such Filmographs
by various institutions through the Filmographing and distributing service of the organization which is contemplating
this unique service.[15]

In France, meanwhile, scholarly micropublishing had become
a reality. The Bureau international de l'edition informed Binkley
in a letter that "filmslide publication books are already being
placed upon a business basis."[16] And another Parisian concern,
Société des éditions sur films des bibliothèques de France, noti-
fied him that it had begun "the publication of certain rare and
valuable books in filmslide form."[17]

Despite these efforts, one serious weakness was to continue to
frustrate the use of microfilm for scholarly purposes. This weakness, which persists today, was the poor quality of the equipment
needed to read microfilm. Binkley described his own difficulties
with both a Leica and a Spencer Lens Company reader:

Both these projectors when used with newsprint reduced
18 diameters will delineate clearly only about one-third to
one-half of the material on the screen. If the center is
brought into focus, the text at the edge of the screen will be
blurred; if the text at the edge is brought into focus, the
center will blur. . . . Both projectors are hot to touch, but
the heat does not seem to damage the film.[18]

There also was the question of standardization (discussed in greater detail in later chapters) which Binkley perceived early on: "If filmslide photography is to attain its maximum usefulness, there must be a standardization of equipment which will make rolls of filmslide interchangeable among institutions using them."[19]

Binkley's conclusions were significant, not because they stimulated a stampede into micropublishing—they did not—but because they put the ACLS and the SSRC on record as advocates of the use of microphotography for research materials. His conclusions were encouraging:

> The technical perfection of the apparatus now on the market is sufficient to recommend it for use in copying all printed and manuscript pages of normal size at costs below normal book prices. The only doubt that can be raised in connection with this use of the method is the question of the durability of the film.[20]

Regarding newspapers, he stated:

> The filmslide method is suited to newspaper copying because it develops its most significant economies in copying very large pages, or in making a small number of copies of a large amount of material. . . . If no effective method of preserving ordinary newsprint is discovered, or if the method should prove to be too expensive for general use, the device which present technology would indicate as most promising as a means of preserving fifty years' legacy of perishable paper is the filmslide copying method.

> The filmslide method also enters into the solution of the newspaper problem as a device for completing files, for improving the distribution of the most important newspaper sets throughout the country, or for saving storage space in crowded libraries.[21]

Asked to continue his work under the sponsorship of the SSRC and ACLS, Binkley produced a second study in 1936 that was published in an edition of 1,500 copies.[22]

There had been a number of intriguing developments by 1936. The New York Times Company, in association with the Joint Committee on Materials for Research, had asked a number of librarians "whether they would prefer, for permanent preservation, the full-size rag paper copy of the *Times* or a rag paper copy reduced one diameter by the photo offset process."[23] A majority of the librarians contacted indicated a preference for the reduced-size format primarily because the advantage if offered in storing and handling outweighed the disadvantages in reading.[24] However, the experiment was dropped because of the libraries' failure to guarantee purchase of the reduced size.[25]

Still another joint committee experiment was conducted in conjunction with the Millar Publishing Company and the Bausch and Lomb Company. Newspapers were reduced to two-thirds of their normal size and read with a direct reading device, "a lens, set in a frame with a curved segment of a cylinder of optical glass mounted about two inches above it, and the whole system set on a swinging arm, made adjustable by means of a screw, to wring over the page at the proper distance for magnifying purposes."[26] Although the approach interested the joint committee, it was not implemented as a commercial venture.

Binkley also reported on a primitive reduction system for dissertations developed in 1933 by Professor Charles C. Peters of Pennsylvania State College. Peters had placed on one side of a page a dissertation abstract printed in pica typescript reduced to about 60 percent of full size; the other side contained a longer abstract reduced to between 5 and 10 percent of normal size.[27]

The early 1930s also brought development of the Fiskoscope, a hand-held reading lens named for its inventor, Admiral Bradley A. Fiske. It was a small binocular lens set in a frame that was held to the eye like a lorgnette. The frame held a long strip of paper that could be moved up or down by the rotation of a ratchet. The text was typewritten in short lines so that about 150 words could be laid on a page, double-spaced.[28] While an ingenious device, the Fiskoscope was exhausting to use.

Another approach to document reproduction came from Atherton Seidell of the U.S. Public Health Service. In the early 1930s, he developed the filmstat, a method that involved reducing book pages by 10 diameters and then reading them with a special magnifier.[29] He also devised a portable microfilm camera which he produced in limited quantities. Rather then sell the cameras, Seidell donated them to libraries on the condition that the recipients agree to provide microfilm copies of specific holdings free of charge upon request to scholars.[30]

And, at the Huntington Library in San Marino, California, Dr. Lodewyk Bendikson used a Leica camera to photograph pages with exposures of 1 × 1¼ inches. Then, he placed a few rows of the film copies side by side in a printing frame and made a positive copy on paper. He used a low-power binocular microscope as his reading device.[31]

In 1935, at Binkley's urging the Joint Committee on Materials for Research sponsored the microfilming of the code hearings of the National Recovery Administration (NRA) and the Agricultural Adjustment Administration (AAA). Binkley saw in this massive project the means of proving the advantages of microphotography to the scholarly community. The nonconfidential records of the two agencies contained invaluable information on business interests and practices in the 1930s, but the cost of publishing all 315,000 pages would have been prohibitive—an estimated half million dollars![32] Even the price of mimeographed copies of the records, estimated at $5,000, was much too high for libraries. The joint committee was able to produce the first ten microfilm copies for $413.50 each, or $13.00 per 100 pages, a dramatically successful demonstration of how economically these otherwise inaccessible materials could be made available to scholars.[33] Again, Binkley expounded upon the need as he saw it:

> To-day the Western scholar's problem is not to get hold of books that everyone else has read or is reading but rather to produce materials that hardly anyone else would think of looking at. That is, of course, the natural consequence of the highly specialized organization of our intellectual activity. As a result, so far as Western Culture is concerned, the qualities of the printing process that began in the fifteenth century to make things accessible have now begun in our different circumstances to make them inaccessible. When

many, if not all scholars wanted the same things, the printing press served them. In the twentieth century, when the
number who want the same things has fallen in some cases
below the practical publishing point (American Indian
language specialists are an illustration), the printing press
leaves them in the lurch. Printing technique, scholarly activities, and library funds have increased the amount of
available material at a tremendous rate, but widening interests and the three-centuries' accumulation of out-of-print
titles have increased the number of desired but inaccessible books at an even greater rate. Scholarship is now ready
to utilize a method of book production that would return to
the cost system of the old copyist, by which a unique copy
could be made to order and a very few reproductions supplied without special expense.[34]

The joint committee then considered an even more ambitious
project, the filming of 2 million pages of books printed in England before 1640. It would have made available to researchers
copies of all books listed in Pollard and Redgrave's *Short Title
Catalogue.*[35]

The scheme was not only more ambitious than the NRA/AAA
project, but also more expensive with the cost of travel, additional
supervision, and the setting and resetting of the camera to photograph random-sized volumes. The project was abandoned when
the joint committee request to film the early English books was
denied, but the idea was a sound one and in 1938 was carried out
by a commercial micropublisher (see Chapter 3).

A more modest joint committee effort was the microfilming of
the papers of Dr. Sidney Mezes in 1935 at the request of Ingram
Bander, an instructor at City College in New York City.[36] Mezes'
papers thus were made available to individuals interested in the
Paris Peace Conference. Binkley expressed hope that the microfilming of Mezes' correspondence would induce others to micro-
publish more important documentary collections.[37]

The next significant development, however, was the 1934 institution of the "Bibliofilm Service" at the U.S. Department of
Agriculture Library. This first "on demand" microfilm service

provided microfilm negatives of books or periodical articles upon request to either individuals or organizations. Atherton Seidell, along with Dr. R. H. Draeger of the U.S. Navy and Claribel Barnett, a librarian at the Department of Agriculture, were the organizers. The new service was described as follows:

> The procedure begins with the suppliance of a 3″ × 5″ slip or card specifying the article desired—one such slip for each and every article, and each slip carrying the name and address of the customer. The slips are returned with the finished films. Attendants take the slips, search the library, send the books to the photographing room; there each article is copied on a continuous strip of film, leaving spaces between for cutting. When all the day's orders are photographed, the film will be developed, fixed, washed and dried, then cut up and each sequence attached to its proper slip and mailed to the customer or delivered by hand as it may be. Prepayment for the service is urged when possible, this to save accounting, etc., and a deposit of funds which may be drawn.[38]

In his 1936 report Binkley emphasized the importance of microphotography to the individual scholar. Although there are few specific examples, it is certain that scholars using Leica cameras were the first to film archival records in connection with their own work. Binkley discussed the value of this new means of assembling research data:

> Just as the scholars of the last generation found in general that it was desirable to be able to use the typewriter, so the scholars of the next generation will find it necessary to use photography. Just as each scholar works out his own note system, combining typescript and longhand notes, so the scholar of the future will make his combinations of typescript, longhand, photographs on paper, and photographs on film. Microcopying, as a technique in the hands of a man who does his own work of photographing and processing, is reduced to its bare material costs. It offers the possibility that a scholar, by purchasing microcopies from

libraries and by making his own microcopies of excerpts
from books, may build up organized accumulations of data
that will resemble a private library in extensiveness, and a
note system in its internal organization. That which scholars
in the past have been able to do with the help of an ama-
nuensis, the scholar of the future may be able to accomplish
with photographic equipment.[39]

In an unused closet near his office at Western Reserve University, Binkley conducted his own microfilming experiments with
a Leica. Eugene Power recalls that Binkley's "enthusiasm and
satisfaction knew no bounds if after swishing a piece of film
though three trays of chemicals, he had a recognizable image. He
was no technician, but his wideranging intelligence did perceive
the tremendous potential use of 35 mm microfilm as a tool of
scholarship."[40] Binkley's enthusiasm extended to the promise of
scholarly micropublishing as it developed in the mid-twentieth
century:

A library with a collection of theatre programs, or pamphlets
of the revolutionary war, or historical manuscripts may
adopt the policy of making microcopies of its material upon
request. If it adopts this policy, its whole collection becomes available to the world as if published. . . . Before the
eyes of scholarship there looms a new unit of intellectual
activity—the making of collections which will be complete
within their predetermined limits to a degree that has been
hitherto impossible. And this new unit, the collection,
ceases to be functionally distinct from a publication. . . .The
more clearly . . . this is achieved, the greater will be the
place that scholarship must give to the bibliographical and
abstracting services that will guide the research worker
through the embarrassing array of materials that will become accessible to him. . . . If manuscript material is
microcopied in Europe and brought to America, it becomes
a new item, a new resource of American scholarship. But
the same is true of a body of American manuscripts that
may be discovered in an attic and deposited in a library
that offers microcopying service.[41]

Binkley's report concluded with the observation that "ordinary commercial publishing will take care of the distribution of any material desired by 2,000 paying customers. But a vast amount of material for scholarly use and a great many of the products of scholarship do not and should not receive such distribution. This is the penalty scholarship must pay for specialization."[42] His solution to this problem was, of course, microphotography. Indeed, the first successful commercial micropublishing firm in the United States, University Microfilms, was founded on the premise that the only efficient means of providing materials needed in small editions was through microphotography.[43] (The founding of University Microfilms is described later in this study.)

The advent of commercial scholarly micropublishing was preceded by Science Service, a Bibliofilm Service program announced in 1936 to the editors of scientific publications as follows:

The development of photographic techniques makes it possible for Science Service to extend to you an invitation to participate in an auxiliary plan of publication which, we believe, will be of aid to you in editing your journal, proceedings or other media of publication, and to scientific publication in general.

You, in common with other scientific editors, are probably under pressure from authors to publish papers of too great length or of too specialized content. Or there are papers that you would like to print in extenso if finances permitted. To a small specialized audience, these papers in complete detail should be made available.

The following suggested procedure will secure effective publication and conserve your finances. It is hoped that you will join with us in putting it into effect.

Publish as much or as little of a paper as you wish in your journal. In the case of a very technical paper, this may be merely an abstract or summary. . . . The author will have his paper typed in an acceptable standard form. . . . This

material will be deposited by you with Science Service as a
document. Science Service will assign a serial document
number and set a price per copy of the document in microfilm or photocopy form. Those who wish to have the document will be able to obtain it by ordering it directly from
Science Service in response to the notice published in your
journal.[44]

Binkley's 1931 report had stressed advances in the mechanics
of microcopying, that is, efficient cameras and readers. By 1936,
however, he wrote confidently that "the mechanical problems
are so well on the road to solution that they need not cause concern."[45] Accordingly, he was now convinced that library
resources could be significantly increased through microfilm. He
concluded his report with the observation that

At the same time the prospect that a scholar may be able to
have material that was otherwise inaccessible brought to
him, and that he may be able to communicate to his colleagues writings that he has hitherto been unable to
communicate to them, open the way to new intellectual
opportunities.[46]

However, even with the proper tools scholars and librarians still
faced the task of insuring that essential records were preserved
via microphotography.
    At this time, scholarly microphotography was confined largely
to the cooperative efforts of foundations and academicians to
film, process, and distribute resources of value to researchers.
The prospect of scholarly micropublishing as a profitable commercial venture had not been considered.
    Binkley himself had no reason to suppose that microfilm proj-
ects would generate interest beyond that of the foundations that
had sponsored the few micropublications available by 1936.
Indeed, the first major microfilming project was financed by a
donation of $490,000 from John D. Rockefeller, Jr. Known only
as "Project A," this massive effort supervised by historian
Samuel Flagg Bemis, resulted in the copying of some two and a
half million pages in Europe, Canada, and Mexico of materials

relating to America which eventually were placed in the Library of Congress.[47]

"Project A" stimulated the establishment of library microfilming facilities at Yale, the Huntington Library, Harvard, and the University of Chicago. In 1933, the Library Journal reported that an American scholar had made films with a Leica camera of materials in twenty-seven libraries in seven European countries.[48]

As "Project A" neared completion, the Recordak Corporation, with eight years of experience filming bank checks and other commercial records behind it, began (with the advice of the New York Public Library) to film the back files of The New York Times.[49] Then, in 1935, during its annual summer conference in Richmond, Virginia, the American Library Association (ALA) officially recognized the significance of micropublication, an event that certainly qualifies as the birth of library microfilming.[50] On the conference agenda was a symposium on microfilm and an exhibit on microfilm cameras and readers.

In a report delivered to the ALA, M. Llewellyn Raney, director of the University of Chicago libraries, expressed concern that lack of standardization in microphotography threatened wider use of microfilm. Raney explained that "at the moment of writing, ther is not in the market a single projector which is capable of handling all films presented it. This arises from a lack of standardization in filming."[51] The standardization problem was not resolved at the 1935 conference. Instead, it became an issue that continued to recur as scholarly micropublishing developed.

However, important action was taken on an equally significant matter when the ALA Executive Board passed a resolution recognizing the legitimacy of microphotography as a research tool.

RESOLVED, That the Executive Board appoint a Committee on Photographic Reproduction of Library Materials, charged with the responsibility of investigation; encouraging experimentation; cooperation with other committees of the A.L.A. and with other agencies; disseminating information; serving in an advisory capacity to librarians and the A.L.A.; and in other ways fostering the appropriate use by libraries of devices which are or may become available for reproduction of library materials.[52]

The ALA action stimulated a number of papers on the subject of documentary microphtography, and in 1938 *The Journal of Documentary Reproduction,* a publication devoted exclusively to the topic, was established under ALA auspices.[53] The following year, the Columbia School of Library Service offered the first course of microphotography.[54] By then, twenty-one different microfilm cameras were available to libraries, enough to prompt this comment by a microphotography expert: "True, some of them were not well suited to the job ahead, and others were custom-made machines; but time promised to take care of that."[55]

Binkley's work with the joint committee had by this time attracted international attention. The director of the National Library in Peking requested the committee's assistance in exhibiting modern library equipment in China. In conjunction with the ALA, Binkley managed to secure a $16,000 contribution from David H. Stevens, head of the Humanities Section of the Rockefeller Foundation, to underwrite a microfilm exhibit at the 1937 Paris Exposition. The exhibit included a complete microphotographic laboratory for demonstration of the filming, development, and processing of newspapers, as well as of film projection equipment. Although Binkley did want to show how microfilm could be used, his primary aim was to help stop a trend in European libraries to favor the photostat over microfilm.[56]

The exhibit did produce some results which David H. Stevens reported to the Rockefeller Foundation Board:

> We now know that costs for foreign work can be kept at certain low prices, and free access has been gained for the first time to the holdings of the Bibliothèque Nationale. During the autumn of 1938, events in Europe unquestionably had their part in increasing the desire of libraries to get their rare materials into microfilm copies. The combination of understanding and need was accidental, but fortunate for the future of library development both here and abroad. We should look toward the easy transfer of materials from country to country and greater security for perishable documents. Also, it is unquestioned that the work at

the National Archives and elsewhere in this country will motivate entirely new standards of library construction so that we shall have fireproof vaults for film and a great saving of space in handling certain classes of documents.[57]

The following year, 1938, brought even more progress, specifically the founding of University Microfilms by Eugene Power in Ann Arbor, Michigan (see Chapter 3 for a complete discussion of this event) and the establishment of the Foreign Newspaper Microfilming Project at Harvard University.[58] Together, they constituted a significant step forward: dissemination of research materials on demand from a central repository had become a reality.[59]

The Foreign Newspaper Microfilm Project was the creation of Keyes D. Metcalf who had become director of the Harvard University Library in 1937. Earlier, while serving as chief of the Reference Department at the New York Public Library, Metcalf had advised the Recordak Corporation on methods on microfilming newspapers for libraries. Under his supervision, the New York Public Library had set up the nation's first microfilm reading room for newspapers using sample Recordak projectors. The effort was such a success that "it may truly be called a landmark in library history."[60]

At Harvard, Metcalf proposed filming foreign newspapers on a large scale on the condition that other libraries agree to purchase positive copies. He listed the following reasons for instituting the project:

1. To arrange a cooperative project with Harvard as the sponsor. The Harvard University Library has had too little to do with cooperative enterprises, and it is desirable for us to take charge of a project.

2. To make arrangements for the preservation of foreign newspapers in research libraries in the United States. One of the weakest spots in these libraries had been their failure to collect adequate files of this material.

3. To help push microphotography. While I am optimistic about its future, I have feared that the whole thing might,

as President Conant has expressed it, bog down, due to the
fact that we are in a vicious circle. Because there were so
few projectors in their hands, libraries have not bought
film; because there was so little film available, libraries
have not bought projectors. The newspaper enterprise provides one very satisfactory way of breaking this vicious
cycle.[61]

With the aid of a $6,000 grant from the Rockefeller Foundation,
the Harvard Faculty, and James Conant, president of Harvard,
the Foreign Newspaper Microfilm Project undertook in 1939 to
film thirty-seven newspapers[62] on a regular basis. Harvard
bought one copy of each film, and other libraries purchased
selections. Except for interruptions during World War II, sixty-
two newspapers were filmed for all or parts of the years
1938–1955.[63]

Another large-scale project was initiated in 1939 at Brown University under the guidance of L. C. Wroth and H. B. Van Hoesen
of the John Carter Brown and John Hay libraries, respectively.
The goal here was to film titles in the Biblioteca Nacional de
Santiago de Chile, the Biblioteca Nacional de Peru, and other
South American libraries. However, the project was abandoned
after five years because of film scarcity and the travel difficulties
imposed by World War II. Later, the Library of Congress printed
catalog cards for the 2,339 titles that were filmed.[64]

An even more massive undertaking was a cooperative effort of
the University of North Carolina and the Library of Congress to
film records of the legislative proceedings of the American colonies, territories, and states, along with statutory laws, constitu-
tional, administrative, executive, court, and a few local records.[65]
Known as the State Records Microfilm Project, it resulted in the
collection of these records on 160,000 feet of film assembled
between 1941 and 1950. (There were several interruptions because of the war.)

Other developments included a German plan to place 500
microfilm readers in libraries to replace interlibrary loan proce-

dures with microfilm copies of requested material.[66] In the United States, one writer optimistically predicted that by 1948 the world would be interconnected by airships that, among other things, would provide unprecedented interlibrary loan service, with two-day delivery of microfilm to any location.[67]

As symbols of the latest in modern technology, microfilms were placed in time capsules buried at the New York World's Fair in 1938 and at Oglethorpe University in Atlanta, Georgia, in 1940.[68]

Although the Belgian team of Goldschmidt and Otlet had envisioned a microphotographic book in 1906 that resembled the modern microfiche, it was not until 1940 that the first sheet mircofilm or "microfiche" was finally produced. Its development had been delayed by the lack of a camera for microfiche production, a situation that was remedied in 1939 by Joseph Goebel, a German engineer.[69] It was clearly an idea whose time had come: within three months of Goebel's achievement, Lucy M. Lewis, director of libraries in the Oregon State system of higher education, and a colleague, Dr. W. Weniger, also built an experimental camera to produce microfiche.[70]

Analyzing the potential of the new microfiche or "sheet microfilm," an American library periodical concluded that it made possible:

> (1) A natural convenient sectionalization of the material; (2) a system of filing which makes every unit immediately accessible; (3) a means of identification which is integral with each unit and can be read without optical aid; (4) a medium more adaptable to handling and processing in small units than ribbon film; and (5) the possibility of an inexpensive reading machine of limited scope and use.[71]

The only disadvantages mentioned were higher manufacturing costs due to an additional cutting operation and higher handling and packing expenses.

The approach of World War II delayed further research and development of the microfiche and postponed its impact on scholarly micropublishing for several years. The progress of scholarly micropublishing was further impeded by Robert Binkley's death from lung cancer in 1940.[72] No one else understood the potential of microform so well. Binkley's success in convincing the academic community of the value of microphotography as a scholarly research tool was due to his own stature as a respected scholar, as well as to his enthusiasm and persistence. No one could replace him, and his death unquestionably delineated the end of an era.

Individual experiments with microforms, along with the development of microfilm services by nonprofit organizations and cooperative publishing efforts of universities and national libraries, had characterized the fledgling scholarly micropublishing industry of the 1930s. The next decade would see the emergence of a group of energetic entrepreneurs seeking to turn scholarly micropublishing into a money-making proposition.

NOTES

1. Elbridge Sibley, *Social Science Research Council, the First Fifty Years* (New York: Social Science Research Council, 1974), p. 2. Representatives of the American Economic Association, the American Sociological Society, the American Statistical Association, the American Anthropological Association, the American Historical Association, and the American Psychological Association joined with the American Political Science Association in 1924 to form the basic structure of the council. The intellectual work for the projects selected by the council is carried out by committees of social scientists (for example, the Joint Committee on Materials for Research). Funding over the years has come from thirty-eight different philanthropic foundations.

2. Pamphlet published by the American Council of Learned Societies, *A Summary Statement of Its Work and Its Plans for a Fiftieth Anniversary Capital Development Program*, 1969, p. 8. The first function of the ACLS was to represent the United States in the International Union of Academies. It continues to represent American scholarship at various international meetings and association conferences. The ACLS, like the SSRC, has representatives from thirty-three national professional and honorary

societies concerned with the humanities and the humanistic aspects of social sciences.

3. Lester Born, "History of Microform Activity," *Library Trends* 8 (1960): 353. Hubbard W. Ballou, "Photography in the Library," *Library Trends* 5 (1956): 277. Robert C. Binkley, *Manual on Methods of Reproducing Research Materials: A Survey Made for the Joint Committee on Materials for Research of the Social Science Research Council and the American Council of Learned Societies* (Ann Arbor, Mich.: Edwards Brothers, 1936), p. 3.

4. Papers of the American Council of Learned Societies, Library of Congress, Washington, D.C., Box B67.

5. Binkley, *Manual on Methods*, p. 3.

6. An entry for Binkley appears in the *Dictionary of American Biography* (Supplement three). The best biographical material is found in *Selected Papers of Robert C. Binkley*, Max H. Fisch, ed. (Cambridge, Mass.: Harvard University Press, 1948), pp. 3–46.

7. Fisch, ed., *Selected Papers*, p. 6. Binkley's interests ranged widely. His published works include *What Is Right with Marriage* (1929), *Responsible Drinking* (1930), and *Realism and Nationalism* (1935).

8. Papers of the American Council of Learned Societies, Box B67.

9. Robert C. Binkley, *Methods of Reproducing Research Materials: A Survey Made for the Joint Committee on Materials for Research of the Social Science Research Council and the American Council of Learned Societies* (Ann Arbor, Mich.: Edwards Brothers, 1931), p. 81. The reader should be careful not to confuse this source with Binkley's later report published in 1936.

10. Ibid., p. 82.
11. Ibid., p. 83.
12. Ibid., p. 84.
13. Papers of the American Council of Learned Societies, Box B67.
14. Binkley, *Methods of Reproducing Research Materials*, p. 99.
15. Ibid., p. 101.
16. Ibid., p. 102.
17. Ibid.
18. Ibid., p. 105.
19. Ibid., p. 107.
20. Ibid., p. 112.
21. Ibid., pp. 113–14.
22. The 1931 report was well received and difficult to obtain since only 100 copies were printed. Demand for the 1936 report was heavy. The print-run was raised to 1,500 copies, and they were all sold within a

year. For additional information, see The Papers of the American Council of Learned Societies, Box B67.

23. Binkley, *Manual on Methods,* p. 115.

24. Ibid. Binkley points out the following essential facts.

The predominance of area costs in the techniques employing the
principles of photography furnishes a constant temptation to reproduce as large a number of words as possible on a given area.
The ease with which an original copy can be reduced in size in the
course of photographic reproduction increases the temptation,
and the mathematical law that utilization of area increases by
squares while reduction of linear dimension of the writing pro-
ceeds arithematically clinches the economy argument in favor of
reducing all texts to the smallest legible size.

25. The overwhelming majority of librarians at this time were in
favor of retaining original issues of a newspaper rather than changing to
reduced-size copies.

26. Binkley, *Manual on Methods,* p. 116.

27. Ibid., p. 117.

28. Ibid.

29. Ibid., p. 118.

30. Interview with Vernon Tate, November 14, 1976.

31. Binkley, *Manual on Methods,* p. 118.

32. The cost of making the master negative, including the renting of
equipment, was $455 for 13,400 feet of 16 mm film.

33. Binkley, *Manual on Methods,* p. 132. The enterprise liquidated
itself completely without expense to the joint committee except for such
costs as were involved in taking up the time of the staff. For additional
information see Papers of the American Council of Learned Societies,
Box B67.

34. Robert C. Binkley, "New Tools for Men of Letters," *Yale Review*
(November 1935): 523.

35. Papers of the American Council of Learned Societies, Box B67.
Additional information on this project is found in Chapter 3.

36. Papers of the American Council of Learned Societies, Box B67.

37. Ibid. Binkley also felt that the Mezes correspondence illustrated
that microfilm could be resorted to when a small body of documents,
about the size of a monograph, was important enough to warrant distribution, but not important enough to render book publication possible.

38. Binkley, *Manual on Methods*, p. 134, and Claribel Barnett, "The Bibliofilm Service," *The Camera* 50 (May 1935): 327.

39. Ibid., p. 159.

40. Eugene Power, "O-P Books: A Library Breakthrough," *American Documentation* 9 (1958): 273.

41. Binkley, *Manual on Methods*, p. 160.

42. Ibid.

43. Interview with Eugene Power, July 20, 1976.

44. Binkley, *Manual on Methods*, p. 192.

45. Ibid., p. 195.

46. Ibid., p. 196.

47. Born, "History of Microfilm Activity," p. 353; E. A. Henry, "Books on Film: Their Use and Care," *Library Journal* 57 (1932): 215; David Weber, "The Foreign Newspaper Microfilm Project," *Harvard Library Bulletin* 10 (1956): 275. For additional information on the Rockefeller Foundation involvement, see Papers of the Rockefeller Foundation, Tarrytown, N.Y., Series 200, Box 208, Folder 2476.

48. R. P. Johnson, "The Use of 35-millimeter Camera in European Libraries," *Library Journal* 60 (April 1, 1935): 294.

49. Weber, "Foreign Newspaper Microfilm Project," p. 275. Ballou, "Photography in the Library," p. 278.

50. Ibid., and the Papers of the Rockefeller Foundation, Series 200, Box 208, Folder 2476. The continuing interest by the Rockefeller Foundation in microphotography is evidenced by the copy of the transcripts of the symposium in the Rockefeller Archives.

51. M. Llewellyn Raney, *Microphotography for Libraries* (Chicago, Ill.: American Library Association, 1936), p. 116.

52. Ibid., p. 121.

53. The joint committee viewed the journal as a natural continuation of the two editions of the *Manual on Methods of Reproduction of Research Materials*.

54. The course was taught by a team of three instructors: Mary Bennett of the Libraries Binding and Photographic Services, Dorothy Litchfield of the Libraries Periodicals and Microfilm Reading Room, and Agnes Townsend of the Barnard Physics Department. The technical principles of photography were taught by Agnes Townsend. Dorothy Litchfield instructed on the use of microfilms in the library, while Mary Bennett concentrated on the applications of document photography. For additional information, see Hubbard Ballou's personal file on the teaching of reprography at Columbia University.

The University of Chicago Graduate Library School initiated a course in microphotography during the summer session of 1939. The course was taught by Herman Fussler, head of the Department of Photographic Reproduction at the University of Chicago Libraries.

55. Ballou, "Photography in the Library," p. 278.

56. Papers of the American Council of Learned Societies, Box B67. Also, a letter from Robert C. Binkley to David H. Stevens dated November 18, 1936, found in Papers of the Rockefeller Foundation, Series 200, Box 208, Folder 2478.

57. Papers of the Rockefeller Foundation, Series 200, Box 208, Folder 2476.

58. For a complete history of this projects, see Weber, "Foreign Newspaper Microfilm Project," pp. 275-81.

59. Allen B. Veaner, *Studies in Micropublishing* (Westport, Conn.: Microform Review, Inc., 1977), p. 175.

60. Weber, "Foreign Newspaper Microfilm Project," p. 276.

61. Letter from Keyes Metcalf to David H. Stevens dated May 16, 1938, found in Papers of the Rockefeller Foundation, Series 200, Box 233, Folder 2784.

62. The newspapers for microfilming were selected by analyzing questionnaires sent to libraries interested in participating in the project and to the faculty of the History Department at Harvard. Fifty newspapers were selected by this process. Of these, thirty-seven agreed to allow Harvard to film them. The papers follow: *La Prensa* (Argentina); *Morning Herald* (Australia); *Neue Freie Presse* (Austria); *L'Independence Belge* (Belgium); *Jornal do Commercio* (Brazil); *Globe and Mail* and *Tribune* (Canada); *China Press* (China); *El Tiempo* (Colombia); *Ceske Slovo* (Czechoslovakia); *Berlingske Tidende* (Denmark); *Action Francaise* and *Le Temps* (France); *Frankfurter Zeitung* and *Volkischer Beobachter* (Germany); *Daily Herald, News Chronicle,* and *Manchester Guardian* (England); *Pesti Hirlap* (Hungary); *Irish Times* (Ireland); *Corriere della Sera* and *Giornale d'Italia* (Italy); *Advertiser* (Japan); *Latvijas Kareivis* (Latvia); *Nieuwe Rotterdamsche Courant* (Netherlands); *Evening Post* (New Zealand); *Aftenposten* (Norway); *El Commercio* (Peru); *La Vangardia* and *Heraldo de Aragon* (Spain); *Aftonbladet* and *Social Demokraten* (Sweden); *Journal de Geneve* and *Neue Zurcher Zeitung* (Switzerland); *Cape Times* (Union of South Africa); *Izvestia* and *Pravda* (USSR). For pricing information, see "Harvard Project and Microfilming Foreign Newspapers," *Journal of Documentary Reproduction* 2 (1939): 41-43.

63. Weber, "Foreign Newspaper Microfilm Project," p. 279. Harvard's control of the project came to an end with the papers issued on

December 31, 1955. The Association for Research Libraries in Washington, D.C., assumed control and changed the structure of the program. A master negative of each newspaper was held for preservation purposes, and a positive copy was made available for borrowing by subscriber libraries.

64. Born, "History of Microform Activity," p. 355.

65. Ibid., p. 352.

66. The term "interlibrary loan" denotes the lending of materials from one library to another. The German idea was based on the theory that, if there were many microfilm readers, much of the library's holdings could be placed on microfilm, thus facilitating the transfer of bulky volumes. The German plan was reported in a communication to David H. Stevens from Herman Fussler of the University of Chicago libraries. See Papers of the Rockefeller Foundation, Series 200, Box 208, Folder 2476.

67. Allen B. Veaner, "Micrographics: An Eventful Forty Years—What Next?," in *Studies in Micropublishing: Documentary Sources, 1853–1976*, Allen B. Veaner, ed. (Westport, Conn.: Microform Review, 1977), p. 467.

68. Ibid., p. 468. A second capsule was buried at the New York World's Fair in 1964. It is located 10 feet from the 1938 capsule. Both are to be opened in the year 6939.

69. Letter from Dr. J. Goebel to Alan Meckler, dated May 23, 1977. Goebel was unaware of the work of Goldschmidt and Otlet. He invented the microfiche so that he could make copies of books that were out of print and too expensive to obtain. See letter from Dr. J. Goebel to Alan Meckler dated May 23, 1977.

70. Veaner, ed., *Studies in Micropublishing*, p. 82.

71. Ralph D. Bennett, "Sheet Microfilm," *Journal of Documentary Reproduction* 3 (1940): 39.

72. In 1948, Luther H. Evans, the librarian of Congress, wrote the following about Binkley's impact on scholarly micropublishing, "Microfilm, when he became interested in it, was a means of recording endorsements on checks; when he left it, it was one of the accepted tools of scholarship." See Fisch, ed., *Selected Papers*, p. xi.

3

THE PIONEERS

The founding of University Microfilms in 1938 by Eugene Power of Ann Arbor, Michigan, marks the beginning of scholarly micropublishing as we know it today. Power was convinced that, despite economic depression in the United States and war in Europe and Asia, the time was right for commercial scholarly micropublishing.[1] At the time, he was employed by the book printing firm of Edwards Brothers, pioneers in the development of offset lithography. In an effort to reduce manufacturing costs, the firm had experimented with a number of book production methods. During the 1930s, printing was based on the large edition sale and its small-unit cost necessary to produce a profit. However, because most scholarly works are highly specialized and cannot be expected to produce large sales, publishing in this field has always been uneconomical. Power's interest in overcoming the financial problems that plagued scholarly publishing eventually led him to explore such reproduction processes as photo offset, multigraph, photostat, and microphotography. Each made the publication of small editions more feasible financially.

Naturally, both Power and Edwards Brothers were vitally interested in the work of the Joint Committee on Materials and Research. In fact, the firm published both of the committee's reports by the photo offset process. Power's interest in microphotography deepened in 1935 when the committee's secretary, Dr. T. R. Shellenberg of the U.S. National Archives, visited

Edwards Brothers. Power later recalled how profoundly his discussions with Shellenberg affected him.

> It was Dr. T. R. Shellenberg who brought the word of microfilms to Ann Arbor, for on a visit early in February, 1935, just after the A.A.A. and N.R.A. code hearings had been microfilmed, he explained to me the remarkable economies possible through the use of this very new technique. For many years Edwards Brothers had been interested in the reproduction of scholarly material in limited quantities, and this new method seemed to fit in perfectly with their program.
>
> A host of uses and applications immediately suggested themselves when an actual film was demonstrated in one of the early Eastman readers, for it seemed obvious that here was a process which would meet a very real need. The main problem involved the selection of a collection of source material for which there would be considerable demand and which would provide a thoroughly satisfactory demonstration of the effectiveness of the new technique.[2]

Soon, Power sought to put some of his ideas to the test. His first venture involved an Edwards Brothers' program offering small editions of out-of-print books (reprints) to the scholarly market. The firm had failed to sell most of the books, and Power thought microfilm would be the most efficient means of making them available. It eliminated the need for large edition printing and allowed for "on demand" publishing: inventory could be produced upon receipt of orders.[3]

Power convinced his employers to experiment and suggested that the first effort be the series of early English books the joint committee had considered filming in 1935. Years later, Power described how the project was selected and the work accomplished.

> For many years Dr. Andrew Keogh, Librarian of Yale University, had dreamed of photostating all the items in Pol-

lard and Redgrave's *Short Title Catalogue* . . . for the use of
the Yale Library and possibly for others who might wish
copies. He had been forced to give up this project as it
would have required at least a quarter of a million dollars
to produce the photostat negative alone. A part of this
immensely valuable collection of source material seemed
the ideal medium for a demonstration of the potentialities
of microfilm. With the help of Dr. W. W. Bishop, Librarian
at the University of Michigan, and an unofficial advisory
committee consisting of Dr. Alfred Potter of Harvard University, Dr. Andrew Keogh of Yale University, and Dr.
H. M. Lydenberg of the New York Public Library, this project was formulated and preliminary arrangements for
work were made with certain European libraries.

At that time the camera developed by Dr. R. H. Draeger
was the only automatic book microfilm camera known and
there were none available on the market. Therefore, it was
necessary to build one. Instead of starting from the beginning, the advice of Mr. Robert Matson of Detroit was followed. He constructed a special camera for the project using
an adopted Universal moving picture camera to which
various parts were added. It is entirely automatic in operation, with a ratio of reduction of from 2:1 to 25:1, and
exposes only a single frame.

During the summer of 1935 I took this camera to England.
Photographers were instructed in its use and arrangements
were made for photographing all books printed in English
before 1550 insofar as they could be located.[4]

Eleven libraries expressed interest in the series and agreed to
purchase the microfilm version at a yearly rate of $500. It took
four years to complete delivery at 100,000 pages per year, at a
cost of approximately one-half cent per page.[5]
  The microfilming operation itself ran smoothly, although
packaging did present a problem. Initially, each microfilm of a
book was delivered in an individual container, sixteen to a box,
that could be stored on a shelf in the same manner as a book.
However, this method proved unwieldy, and subsequent ship-

ments were in rolls of approximately 100 feet of film, six rolls per buckram case.[6]

After the first year's work was completed, Power observed:

> Thus far, 63,000 pages have been delivered and there is sufficient negative material in the United States of which positives are now being made to supply more than the additional 40,000 pages. This will be delivered within the next six weeks or two months, as rapidly as positives can be made, thus completing the amount of material to be delivered during the first year. There have been certain delays which were unavoidable, both in the making of the negatives in England and in the making of the positives in this country. A considerable amount of experimentation has been done with this latter problem with the result that we now feel we can produce a positive which is clear, sharp, and for most purposes, a satisfactory substitute for the original book.
>
> . . . We have learned much by way of making negatives and positives, and in presenting, storing, and cataloging them. The coming year should go much smoother. It has been suggested that during this year we consider filming not only books printed in English but all books printed in England before 1550 irrespective of the language, which will round out this collection of material.[7]

The success of the program eventually demanded a separate organization within Edwards Brothers to handle the increased workload. Normal book production procedures were not compatible with microfilm manufacturing, which required processing of the positive copies (duplicates or copies that were being shipped to the subscribers) made from the negatives produced in England.

By 1938, however, the firm had decided that its future lay in book production, not micropublishing. As a result, Power acquired all of the Edwards Brothers' microfilm business, including the name University Microfilms, its contracts, subscriptions, and equipment in the United States and abroad. And so, at thirty-three, Power was on his own. His first child had been born three days after he acquired University Microfilms. His first office consisted of two rooms at the back of an Ann Arbor funeral parlor. But he never doubted his future; University Microfilms showed a profit in 1938 and every year thereafter.[8]

In 1939, the new firm began to provide a unique service: the filming of doctoral dissertations which it then sold upon demand. The need, as Power saw it at the time, was obvious.

> The development of the microfilm technique has opened the way to what may be the solution of another serious and difficult problem, namely, the publication of contemporary manuscripts for which demand is too small to justify usual methods of reproduction. University Microfilms has attempted to solve this problem in a way which differs from any of the usual publishing techniques. . . .

> For 50 years at least the publishing of dissertations has been a serious problem. Many solutions, ranging from full publications with letterpress printing to miniature offset prints and the deposition of manuscripts in the library for loan, have been tried. All of these methods have, in various institutions, been considered as fulfilling the publication requirements for the doctorate, but none has proved entirely acceptable.

> There are many factors which lie back of the need for another method of publication of thesis material. Basically, the need arises from the fact that all our reproductive processes are designed to produce copies economically only when a large number are needed. If but a dozen copies of a manuscript are printed, the cost per copy is exceedingly high. It is this factor which has resulted in the current publishing philosophy, whereby one estimates as accurately as possible the potential sale, prepares that number and hopes that sufficient books will be sold to cover at least the initial investment. This is often a vain hope as indicated by the results of recent surveys, which reveal that on an average

less than one half of the editions of scholarly publications are sold. This means, of course, that unsold stock represents an investment which can never be recovered and this is a very real loss of the total funds of scholarship.

Roughly speaking, the publishing function can be broken down into two broad divisions of activity: notification, or the process of advising the prospective purchaser of what is offered, and distribution, the delivery of a copy of the book or manuscript upon request. The process of notification involves very little investment, but because printing facilities are so constructed that it is necessary to print a large number of copies at one time, a considerable investment is required before it is possible to deliver a single copy.

From the foregoing it would seem that the ideal solution would be one whereby the process of notification is adequately carried out and copies of the manuscript are produced upon demand. Under such a plan the investment in any title would be small since there would be no stock to be produced in advance. Microfilm offers exactly this possibility in an effective and economical form.

He also outlined a plan that was implemented then and that slightly altered, remains in operation today.

1.   The author will submit with a first copy of his manuscript an approved abstract of approximately 500 words describing briefly his methods and results. The manuscript is microfilmed and returned to the author, and the negative is kept on file at University Microfilms in Ann Arbor.

2.   The abstract is printed in a booklet of abstracts, and distributed to leading libraries, journals, and the current bibliographies without cost to the recipients. Printed library catalog cards for each abstract accompany the booklet. This completes the process of notification.

3.   A scholar working in a given field will locate a reference to the titles listed either in the card catalog file, in his jour-

nals or the current bibliographies, which will refer him to
an abstract giving a fairly comprehensive idea of the contents of the original manuscript. Should it seem, upon
examination of the abstract, that the original manuscript
would be of use to him, he can secure a positive microfilm
copy of it from the filed negative at the rate of one and one
fourth cents per page.

4.   Any material published in this form is eligible for copyright protection and should it prove, through experience,
that there is a considerable demand, publication may be
arranged through any of the usual channels. In other
words, there are no restrictions upon the author covering a
subsequent and further publication of material originally
published in microfilm form.

Power concluded his description of the new program with this
summation of its advantages:

Here is an effective solution to the problem of thesis publication which makes possible the distribution of material
adequately and economically, not only in this country but
abroad as well, which does not place an excessive burden
upon the candidate. . . . The method involves a new princi-
ple in publishing, that of production upon demand, and of
limiting the investment in any given title. It can make possible more effective use of the total available funds of
scholarship than ever before, and, at the same time, will
release the individual scholar from the limitations which
highly mechanical printing presses have placed upon the
distribution of his material.[9]

   Power's first step was to present his concept to Clarence
Yokum, dean of the Graduate School at the University of Michigan. Dean Yokum was so enthusiastic about the project that he
offered to supply University Microfilms with dissertations from
the University of Michigan.[10] Next, Power sought to provide a
microfilm service that made available to scholars materials in
European libraries. He received a grant-in-aid from the Carnegie

Corporation to establish filming operations at various libraries in England (he already had facilities at the British Museum for the early English books project) and elsewhere in Europe. Although the outbreak of World War II curtailed his plans somewhat, he was able to involve several important libraries in the project. He described the need for the service and its mode of operation:

> Probably the fact of greatest interest to American scholarship is the existence of a service whereby microfilm may be secured upon individual order from the principal libraries of England, Holland, Belgium, France, Switzerland, Italy, and Germany. These libraries were visited, the usability of microfilm and the needs of American scholars were explained, and facilities were either set up or arranged, so that copies of the contents of these depositories may now be secured by any American scholar who has a legitimate use for them.[11]

Power arranged with the participating libraries for University Microfilms to serve as a central ordering, shipping, and billing agency. Even direct orders to foreign libraries would be shipped first to University Microfilms and then to the customer. Without exception, the libraries Power contacted were receptive to requests from American scholars.[12]

Initial orders filled by University Microfilms included the following:

Germany, four reels
Belgium, one reel
France, eight reels
Italy, thirteen reels
England, twenty-two reels

Thus, materials from European libraries found their way to forty-eight scholars in the United States who then could use them in their own libraries.[13]

Although Americans were receptive to the use of microfilm for scholarly work, the same could not be said of Europeans, as Power observed:

It should be realized, however, that as distances are usually
short and as the European scholar is conservative by nature,
microfilm will not be accepted as quickly there as here;
and for some time to come these countries will doubtless
remain sources rather than users of microfilm. However,
some European libraries and certain scholars are keenly
aware to the possibilities of the technique, and are interested
in developing its use in their own countries.[14]

Just before World War II erupted, Power filmed the manuscript
catalog of the holdings of the Convent of San Marco to test his
conviction that still another important use of microfilm was the
reproduction of unpublished catalogs: "Microfilm offers an
inexpensive and practical method of augmenting bibliographical
holdings in America, which combined with adequate facilities
for reproducing texts makes the contents of great libraries available to the American scholar.[15]

By the end of 1939, Power had firmly established University
Microfilms as America's first and foremost scholarly micropublisher. With boldness and entrepreneurial initiative he had
created a small micropublishing empire, and he had conclusively
demonstrated that reproducing research materials on microfilm
for specialized markets was indeed a viable business.

ALBERT BONI AND READEX MICROPRINT

After twenty years in book publishing, Albert Boni, at the age
of forty, turned his attention to micropublishing. In 1912, Boni
had launched his career by founding, with his younger brother
Charles, the Washington Square Bookshop in New York City.[16]
They also published a number of books, including Will Durant's
little-known *Socialism and Anarchism*.[17] In another notable venture, Boni and Harry Scherman, who was to become the founder
of the Book of the Month Club, jointly created in 1915 the "Little
Leather Library." They issued books bound in lambskin by such
authors as Oscar Wilde, George Bernard Shaw, William Shake-
speare, and Elizabeth Barrett Browning.[18] Two years later, Boni
formed yet another partnership, this time with Wall Street spec-

ulator Horace Liveright, to promote a book series called the "Modern Library."

From its inception, the firm made money and by December 1918 had produced a profit of $8,000 on an investment of $16,500.[19] The "Modern Library" books were bound in imitation leather and sold at 60 cents apiece. Among the sixty titles issued during the first two years were reprinted works by Oscar Wilde, George Bernard Shaw, Thomas Hardy, Anatole France, H. G. Wells, Anton Chekov, and William Dean Howells, as well as original books by Theodore Dreiser and Leon Trotsky. Financial conflicts and personal arguments eventually undermined the partnership, and in 1921 Boni sold his interest to Liveright.

In 1924, Boni embarked on another publishing venture with his brother Charles, founding the firm A & C Boni. Although they were to publish works by a distinguished group of writers, including Will Rogers, Upton Sinclair, James Gould Cozzens, Marcel Proust, and Thornton Wilder, the Bonis, as many publishers, were severly affected by the Great Depression. Although their imprint survived, it did little more than languish during the 1930s.[20]

By 1932, Boni himself was anxious for a new challenge. Then, at a party, he was shown an album of photographs his host had made with a Leica camera. The first picture was a contact print of a man sitting in a chair. It was followed by a series of enlargements of increasingly small areas of the original negative. The last was a 4 × 5 inch print of a corner of the subject's eye. Boni was astounded by the fine detail.[21] He immediately grasped the potential of using the enlargement process in reverse and, completely unaware of microphotographic developments, began to explore the space-saving possibilities of microfilm. He concluded that what was needed was a process to combine photographic reduction and printing into a new microformat.

Boni understood that there was no problem in obtaining the image of a printed page on film. The challenge lay in transferring the original negative to a printing plate and then, from the plate, to produce an impression that under suitable magnification would be both legible and durable. He wanted to accomplish with a printing press what already was possible photographically.[22]

For the next seventeen years Boni worked on his microprint process.[23] Microprint is a method of reproducing books or other documentary material in reduced facsimile in the form of a paper print. The paper print or microprint measures 6 × 9 inches and contains 100 facsimile pages each measuring 0.5 × 0.8 inches. The pages are consecutively arranged in ten rows of ten pages per row reading from right to left. Each microprint contains the title page of a book or some other identifier that can be read by the naked eye.[24]

Boni contended that microprint would be more convenient to use and file than microfilm. Since it was in the form of paper prints, he reasoned that scholars and other users could handle it in much the same manner as other printed documents.[25] He also thought microprint was more economical than microfilm for producing editions of twenty-five copies or more. In the microfilm process, production and materials costs are constant. With microprint, however, although there are larger costs for making plates and preparing a printing press, production of new editions in any quantity can be accomplished at a consistently decreasing cost.[26]

Boni's first major Readex Microprint project, the complete British House of Commons *Sessional Papers,* resulted from a 1940 meeting with Edgar L. Erickson, professor of history at the University of Illinois. Erickson, who was chairman of the Publications Committee of the American Historical Association, had been looking for an economically feasible means of reissuing the *Sessional Papers.*[27] There was, however, a considerable obstacle to the project. Nowhere in the world—not even in the House of Commons itself, or in the British Museum—was there a single complete collection of the papers. To carry out the project, a staff assembled and supervised by Professor Erickson worked for ten years in the New York Public Library to locate, collect, and collate the papers, assign page numbers and, finally, photograph them.[28]

While the editorial work on the *Sessional Papers* progressed, Readex offered its first publications, four bibliographical works known by their compilers' names: Sabin, Evans, Church, and

Harrissee. The combined set (fifty volumes) was priced at $85; several hundred were sold.[29] The Readex production process was adequate for short bibliographical collections, but not for the large initial print runs of the *Sessional Papers*. The special quality of paper required for microprint presented problems; the process could not accommodate any variation in paper thickness. Only very slight pressure can be tolerated under the microprint plate when it comes in contact with the paper. War-time shortages of various photographic supplies also prevented Boni from perfecting the Readex process for long-run publications for several years.

Ultimately, the answer to his problem was a new, highly glazed paper called Kromekote developed in 1949 by the Champion Paper and Pulp Company. Its thickness met the requirements of the Readex process, and it could accept ink with very little running. It also met the National Bureau of Standards' requirements for archival paper.[30] All told, it took Boni seventeen years of experimentation to perfect the Readex Microprint. By then, however, another microform—the microcard—had arrived.

FREMONT RIDER AND THE MICROCARD

Fremont Rider's[31] contribution to scholarly micropublishing grew out of his experience as librarian at Wesleyan University in Middletown, Connecticut. He had reason to be alarmed by the growth of research library collections: at Wesleyan, the stacks were filled to capacity a mere ten years after the new library opened.[32] Rider eventually wrote a book on the growth of library research collections, *The Scholar and the Future of the Research Library*, published in 1944. The first section of the book presents his analysis of collection growth and demonstrates, on the basis of a mathematical formula he devised, that research library holdings were doubling every sixteen years. "The scholar," he wrote, "either initiated or accelerated this growth."[32] The second section of the book advanced and elaborated upon his solution—the microcard.

Rider's microcard has some characteristics in common with the microprint. Both rely on microfilm produced by conventional means. With the microprint, the microfilm becomes one page of film printed in ink on one side of a 6 × 9 inch sheet of special paper. Microcards, however, require a special, fine grain, high contrast photographic paper on which contact prints from the microfilm are placed. Each card measures about 3 × 5 inches. The number of pages varies according to the size of the original, but there are no less than thirty nor more than fifty pages per microcard.

Rider's preference for the microcard derived from his conviction that no other microform could be integrated properly with library practices. He used the following example to illustrate the problem as he saw it.

> Some months ago we here at Wesleyan bought from Readex Microprint Corporation their reproduction of the two English literature volumes of the *Church Catalog*. Their microprint copy of these two volumes came to us on six leaves of paper, each leaf six-by-nine inches in size and each printed on both sides. . . . So far as storage was concerned our six leaves of micro-printed *Church Catalog* were delivered to us in a complete unit in a form that negatived practically all of the saving in storage cost that micro-reduction had effected. We were, to all intents and purposes, put right back where we started; we were asked to handle and store a ''book'' again.[34]

To overcome these difficulties, Rider proposed that the microcard serve as a catalog card. In addition to the usual bibliographic entry, it would contain the microtext of the book to which the cataloging information referred. Thus, by locating the card, the reader would also locate the book itself (in microtext). His argument was persuasive:

> Why might we not combine the micro-texts of our books and the catalog cards for these same books in one single entity? In other words, why could we not put our micro-

books on the backs of their own catalog cards? And wasn't this that new "integration" of our basic materials that I had for years been looking for? I called this new concept, this new correlation of functions, a microcard. . . . The more I considered this new microcard idea, the more it grew on me. For, with almost miraculous simplicity, it seemed, automatically, to solve, not one, but all four of the factors of our growth problem.[35]

Thus, he felt it would satisfy the scholar's needs:

In all the endeavors that we may make to solve the problem of research library growth we must always remember that no solution is going to be entirely satisfactory to the scholar if, directly or indirectly, it takes his books away from him. Having the text of his material conveniently near his elbow is his *sine qua non.*

To Rider, the microcard was more than a space-saver; it was a means for libraries to begin anew.

No one seems to have realized that, abruptly, for the first time in over two thousand years, libraries *were being offered the chance to begin all over again.* In this first half of the twentieth century A.D. the recorded words of men were coming in to us for two milleniums, but in a brand new form, an utterly, completely, basically different form, a form that demanded and that, if we could only see it, would require an utterly and completely and basically different library treatment.[36]

A review of Rider's book in *Time* magazine caught the attention of Charles Gelatt, head of the Northern Engraving Company of LaCrosse, Wisconsin. Gelatt, whose company produced engravings on metal, was a regent of the University of Wisconsin, and, as such, was very much aware of library expenditures. He contacted Rider, and in 1948 the two formed the Microcard Corporation based in LaCrosse. The company designed, built, and marketed readers for the microcard as well as equipment for manufacturing microcards.[37]

At the same time, Rider established the Microcard Foundation in Middletown for the purpose of selecting and acquiring books and other research materials to be placed on microcards. The foundation, a nonprofit organization, also provided advice to commercial and noncommercial publishers seeking to enter the microcard field and served as a clearinghouse for all available microcard titles. Its charter also enabled it to provide cataloging advice or actually perform the cataloging for other microcard publishers.[38]

Gelatt provided the foundation with $100,000 in 1949. First-year sales were minimal, primarily because only twenty-six microcard readers had been manufactured. As the number of readers increased, microcard sales expanded.

Alex Baptie, an executive with the Microcard Corporation who worked with Rider, recalls that as businessmen he and Gelatt were completely dependent on Rider's title selection and on his evaluation of the microcard as superior to other microforms. After some research of his own, however, Baptie concluded that the microfiche was preferable to the microcard. Like the micro-print, the microcard required reflex projection which is inferior to the direct projection possible with the microfiche. It had also become apparent that the microcard was not workable for cataloging. Since catalog cards are strung on metal rods slipped through a perforation, it was impossible for users to remove the microcards without dismantling the card catalog drawer. Then, too, as the demand for paper copies of microforms escalated, the lack of a reader/printer to make quality paper copies from microcards (or microprints) soured Baptie and Gelatt on the microcard. However, not until five years after Rider's death in 1965 was the microcard abandoned in favor of the microfiche.[39]

MICROPHOTOGRAPHY AND WORLD WAR II

Microphotography proved a valuable and efficient tool during World War II. Because of the work of libraries and scholarly organizations in the 1930s, microphotographic developments in the United States had far surpassed those of other countries.[40] Thus, in war-time they made possible the preservation of original manuscripts, archives, rare books, personal papers, and even business documents considered at risk. This "insurance copy-ing" of textual material was designed to protect against losses due to damage from bombing or other war-time disaster.[41] With the aid of a $100,000 grant from the Rockefeller Foundation[42] at the outset of the war, the ACLS established a committee "to plan a project whose dual purpose was to preserve from the hazards of war the contents of valuable historical, scientific and literary manuscripts in European repositories, and to provide American scholars with important research materials for research."[43] The importance of the committee's activities was underscored in a letter from President Franklin D. Roosevelt to the president of the Society of American Archivists:

> At this time, and because of the conditions of modern war against which none of us can guess the future, it is my hope that the Society of American Archivists will do all that is possible to build up an American public opinion in favor of what might be called the only form of insurance that will stand the test of time. I am referring to the duplication of records by modern processes like the microfilm so that if any part of the country's original archives are destroyed, a record of them will exist in some other place.[44]

The ACLS formed a subcommittee to prepare consolidated want lists based on hundreds of requests from scholars in various fields for archives in Great Britain and on the European continent. The spread of the war, however, precluded filming in Europe, and the program became known as the British Manuscripts Project.[45]

Filming took place between 1941 and 1945, and the Library of Congress completed cataloging in 1948.[46] The Department of Agriculture's Bibliofilm Service initially was to handle the film-ing, but it was unable to do the work and Eugene Power took over. He was the logical replacement because of his vast experi-ence filming in major English libraries during the 1930s. Power's first step was to ship three microfilm cameras to England to speed up the project, but the boat carrying them was sunk by a German torpedo.[47] Despite difficult war-time conditions, Power eventually managed to film five million pages of manuscripts on 2,600 reels of microfilm.[48]

The government found other uses for microfilm during the war. The National Archives initiated its own microfilm activities in 1939; the War Department filmed enormous amounts of material; and the Navy Department microfilmed nearly two million pages of manuscripts which were deposited in the Office of Naval Records and Library.[49]

During the war, defense contractors began ''to microfilm blue-print files, contract documents, research information, specifications and other vital data''[50]—primarily to protect against accident or bombing. But it also proved a space-saver: a Navy PBY4 bomber required 92,000 separate blueprints which could be reduced to seven rolls of microfilm.[51] Many of the plans for warships damaged at Pearl Harbor were microfilmed and flown to Honolulu. Sending the originals by air would have required a number of transport planes, and sending them by ship would have taken too much time. Microfilm thus facilitated prompt reconstruction of vitally needed warships.[52]

Official correspondence and documentation were similarly transported, and here, again, Eugene Power played a crucial role. While working with the manuscript program, he was asked to assist the Office of the Coordinator of Information (later the Office of Strategic Services) in filming enemy documents obtained by the British for shipment to the United States. Power and his crew were given only twenty-four hours' notice each time they were asked to film documents en route to Washington.[53]

One of the most celebrated microphotographic enterprises was V Mail, a correspondence service for soldiers. Letters were written on prepared forms, which then were microfilmed on 16 mm film to be processed and forwarded by air to a central point. Each reel of film contained about 4,000 letters. At the central point, enlargement prints on paper were made, trimmed, placed in envelopes, and sent on to the addressees.[54]

World War II, then, secured for microphotography a valued role in records-keeping in both government and industry. It broadened awareness of the advantages of microphotography and helped speed the improvement of both processing and reading equipment. It also resulted in the filming of enormous quantities of manuscripts and other documents to be used by researchers for years to come. Librarians, too, became more aware of the benefits of microphotography. Clearly, the war fostered development of all phases of micrographics.

MICRO PHOTO: LAST OF THE EARLY PUBLISHERS

Shortly after the war ended, Samuel Freedman and Leonard Glueck left the Systems Division of the Remington Rand Corporation to form the Micro Photo Company of Cleveland, Ohio. Freedman and Glueck sensed that microphotography of industrial records was a field with a bright future and set out to enter it with a service bureau for filming records, invoices, and other commercial documents.[55] However, they met with little success: many of their potential customers already had contracted with other bureaus. Later, in 1946, after having been hired to film the back issues of a local newspaper, Freedman and Glueck stumbled on the information that the majority of American newspapers had not filmed their current or back issues, and that newspapers and libraries alike faced the problem of deteriorating back files.[56]

Freedman wasted no time. He took the back seat out of his car, put in a microfilm reader, and set off across the country to sign up as many newspapers as possible. This effort met with more success. Micro Photo secured the rights to microfilm back and current issues of most of the papers Freedman visited. The firm also got the rights to the master negative and became the papers' exclusive sales agent. (Micro Photo also offered microfilm editions of defunct newspapers.) By 1950, it held the microfilm rights to nearly 80 percent of the more significant daily newspapers in the United States.[57]

By this point, scholarly micropublishing had become a small but flourishing industry. University Microfilms, Readex Microprint, the Microcard Corporation, and Micro Photo, as well as a few other organizations, marketed copies of monographs, dissertations, manuscripts, and newspapers to libraries and scholars all over the world. Institutions, including the National Archives, the Library of Congress, Harvard University, and various societies were actively involved in noncommercial micropublishing.

Both users and publishers had begun to argue the merits of the available formats: 35 mm microfilm versus the micro-opaques (the microprint and microcard). Soon, the microfiche would gain adherents, and, despite the fact that scholars still preferred hard copy to film, a battle of formats was in the making.

Microphotography had earned both success and notoriety, primarily through the support of a small fraternity of librarians, including Keyes Metcalfe of the New York Public Library and later of Harvard University; Fremont Rider; Vernon Tate of the Massachusetts Institute of Technology (and editor of *The Journal of Documentary Reproduction*, 1938–1942, which supplied the only continuous flow of articles on scholarly micrographics during its infancy); Herman Fussler of the University of Chicago; and many others. With additional support from enlightened academics, these librarians helped launch the new industry by purchasing what the fledgling micropublishers had to sell.

Problems remained, of course. Then, as now, the inadequacy of micrographics equipment discouraged many prospective users of microforms. One writer of the time complained that "reading by means of a mechanical contrivance is so new and so unprecedented in the entire history of writing and printing that it introduces, in addition to its real and obvious difficulties, those of a psychological nature on the part of the prospective reader."[58]

Micrographics equipment manufacturers had scant incentive to develop equipment especially for researchers. Scholarly uses of microphotography could not compare in dollars and cents terms to the tremendous commercial market. Therefore, equipment had been designed primarily to serve the greatest need—that of clerks, not of scholars.

NOTES

1. Interview with Eugene Power, July 20, 1976.
2. Eugene Power, "University Microfilms," *Journal of Documentary Reproduction* 2 (1939): 21.
3. Interview with Eugene Power, July 20, 1976.
The following data prepared by Robert C. Binkley demonstrate the efficiency of microfilm:

PROCESS	EFFICIENCY POINT	COST OF 100,000 WORDS
Printing	2,100 copies	$ 0.58
Mimeoform	1,300 copies	0.42
Photo offset, with typescript composition in a format equivalent to a 7 point type	1,100 copies	0.77
Photo offset, in a reprint book	800 copies	0.50
Mimeograph, in a 300 word per page format	450 copies	0.64
Hectography, including cost of typing fair copy	87 copies	1.58
Hectograph, without composition costs	50 copies	1.00
Micro-copying, long runs	2 copies	0.77
Blueline print	2 copies	19.53
Photostat positive	2 copies	100.23

4. Power, "University Microfilms," pp. 21–22.

5. By the second year of operation, sixteen libraries joined the program. The sixteen were Yale University Library, Harvard College Library, University of Rochester, University of Michigan, Duke University, the Library of Congress, New York Public Library, University of Virginia, University of Illinois, University of Chicago, Boston Public Library, University of Pennsylvania, Public Library of Toronto, University of California at Berkeley, University of Texas, and a joint participation from Mount Holyoke, Smith, and Amherst colleges. Eugene Power, "Report of Progress on Filming English Books Before 1550," *Journal of Documentary Reproduction* 1 (1938): 45.

6. Power, "Report of Progress," p. 46.

7. Ibid., p. 49. Another problem Power encountered was the order in which the books appeared. Originally, the titles were to appear chronologically by year and alphabetically by author and in a sequence similar to Pollard and Redgrave's *Short Title Catalogue*. However, it was impossible to follow the order as given in Pollard and Redgrave. The reason was that certain books became available for microfilming before others, because of location in different libraries.

8. Interview with Eugene Power, July 20, 1976.

9. Power, "University Microfilms," pp. 24–28.

10. Interview with Eugene Power, July 20, 1976.

11. Eugene Power, "Microfilm in Europe, 1939," *Journal of Documentary Reproduction* 2 (1939): 254.

12. There were some restrictions. Foreign libraries wanted to know for whom the material was intended; the purposes for which it was to be utilized; and if publication was intended.

13. Power, "Microfilm in Europe," p. 256.

14. Ibid., p. 258.

15. Ibid.

16. Boni sold his interest in the bookshop in 1917.

17. The book was based on lectures Durant had given at the Ferrar School in Manhattan. The institution was dedicated to an anarchist philosophy that there should be no institutions. See draft of unpublished *New Yorker* "Profile" of Albert Boni, p. 10.

18. Nearly one million books were sold in the first year (1915), of which about 800,000 were disposed of by mail order. The purchaser paid by installments totaling $19.95 (the bookstore price was about one half the installment price). Boni disliked the installment plan. He felt the mail subscriber was being cheated. Eventually, Boni sold his interest to Scherman. See unpublished "Profile," pp. 15–17.

19. Unpublished "Profile," p. 19. The most detailed account of the launching of this series appears in John Tebbel, *A History of Book Publishing in the United States,* Vol. 2 (New York, R. R. Bowker, 1975), pp. 390–92.

20. The last title issued was in 1935.

21. Interview with Albert Boni, November 16, 1976.

22. Unpublished "Profile," p. 97.

23. Charles Farnsley, a practicing lawyer of Louisville, Kentucky, read about Boni's work on developing the microprint. After serving as mayor of Louisville, he started his own micropublishing business in 1955. Because he was not able to learn the "secrets" of the microprint process, he began his business using microcards. (A switch to microfiche was made in 1960.) His first project was titled "Kentucky Culture," comprised of fourteen titles selected by Lawrence Thompson, the librarian at the University of Kentucky. Interestingly, Thompson would later start his own micropublishing firm called Erasmus Press. Interview with Charles Farnsley, October 9, 1978.

24. For additional information, see John Tennant, "Readex Microprints," *Journal of Documentary Reproduction* 3 (1940): 69.

25. Ibid.

26. As the size of the edition is increased, the economies also increase. As the number of copies rises, the production costs are reduced dramatically.

27. Unpublished "Profile," p. 104.

28. Ibid., p. 105.

29. Ibid., p. 106.

30. In order to qualify as "archival," a paper must, under analysis, be capable of surviving 300 years or more.

31. The Fremont Rider Papers are located at the Godfrey Memorial Library in Middletown, Connecticut. The librarian, Doris Post, would not allow this writer to study the Rider Papers.

32. Fremont Rider, *And Master of None* (Middletown, Conn.: Godfrey Memorial Library, 1955), p. 201.

33. Ibid., p. 203.

34. Fremont Rider, "The Future of the Research Library," *College & Research Libraries* 5 (1944): 303.

35. Ibid., p. 307.

36. Ibid., p. 301.

37. Interview with Alex Baptie, November 17, 1976.

38. Rider, *And Master of None,* p. 205.

39. Interview with Alex Baptie, November 17, 1976.

40. Vernon Tate, "Microphotography in Wartime," *Journal of Documentary Reproduction* 4 (1942): 129.

41. Ibid., p. 130.

42. An internal Rockefeller Foundation memo on the reasons behind the grant notes that "The British are naturally interested in the success of the project, for it provides a safeguard against the complete loss of these records, even though the originals should be destroyed as the treasured books in the Royal College of Physicians Library were recently destroyed." For additional information, see Papers of the Rockefeller Foundation, Tarrytown, N.Y., Series 200, Box 196, Folder 2356.

43. Lester Born, "History of Microform Activity," *Library Trends* 8 (1960): 353.

44. Tate, "Microphotography in Wartime," p. 130.

45. For additional information, see Papers of the American Council of Learned Societies, Library of Congress, Washington, D.C., Box J6. See also Papers of the Rockefeller Foundation, Series 200, Box 196, Folder 2356.

46. Born, "History of Microform Activity," p. 354.

47. A checklist was published in 1955.

48. Interview with Eugene Power, July 20, 1976.

49. Born, "History of Microform Activity," p. 354.

50. Tate, "Microphotography in Wartime," pp. 132.

51. Interview with Vernon Tate, November 14, 1976.

52. "Microphotography in Wartime," p. 134.

53. Interview with Eugene Power, July 20, 1976. The Association of Research Libraries advised Power in this activity through its Joint Com-

mittee on Reproduction of Enemy Publications. For additional information, see Papers of the Association of Research Libraries, Washington, D.C., 1944.

54. Interview with Vernon Tate, November 14, 1976. Tate, "Microphotography in Wartime," p. 133.

55. Interview with Samuel Freedman, August 12, 1976.

56. Ibid.

57. Ibid.

58. Herman Fussler, "Microfilm and Libraries," in *Acquisition and Cataloging of Books,* William Madison Randall, ed. (Chicago: University of Chicago Press, 1940), p. 346.

4

THE GROWTH OF SCHOLARLY MICROPUBLISHING

The growth of the micropublishing industry continues today at a healthy pace. It is comprised of some 290 different firms with sales to libraries that reached $55.4 million[1] in 1976-1977, and then jumped to $70 million in 1977-1978.[2] This rapid growth can be accounted for by a number of factors in addition to the continued innovation and entrepreneurial initiatives of men like Eugene Power, Samuel Freedman, and Fremont Rider. Among them were the adoption of microforms as a means of duplicating and disseminating federal government documents, continued foundation support for scholarly projects, technological advances, and the proliferation of new colleges and universities.

This chapter reviews the most significant events in the development of scholarly micropublishing since the end of World War II. Of these, certainly the most far reaching were federal government commitments to microform use for duplicating masses of documents. One of the first agencies to adopt microforms for this purpose was the Atomic Energy Commission (AEC) which contracted with the Microcard Corporation in 1952 to publish all its reports.[3] During the subsequent twelve years (1952-1964), 20 million microcards were distributed.[4] The AEC had determined that microcards rather than microfilm were better suited to the presentation of its reports because of their "individual unit nature." In 1964, however, the agency discarded the format and adopted the microfiche.[5] The switch was made for two reasons: first, because the microfiche made possible better quality paper prints than microcards, and second, because other federal agencies by then had selected the 4 × 6 inch fiche as the standard format for report distribution.[6]

Foreign government agencies soon followed suit. In the mid-1960s, both the British atomic energy agency and the Canadian defense research board adopted the microfiche for dissemination of their reports. In the United States, nongovernmental organizations began opting for the microfiche after 1966 when the transactions of the Society of Automotive Engineers first appeared on microfiche.[7]

More recently, the U.S. Government Printing Office (GPO) initiated a micropublishing program utilizing fiche to distribute government documents to depository libraries. Begun as an experiment in 1974, the program was expanded in 1977 upon instructions from Senator Howard Cannon (D-Nevada), chairman of the Joint Committee on Printing:

1) To convert to microfiche, as necessary and as requested by individual depository libraries, that category of publications identified as "non-GPO documentation."[8]

2) To convert to microfiche, as necessary and as requested by individual depository libraries and when savings in cost are clearly demonstrable, that category of publications identified as "GPO documentation."[9]

Cannon's decision was based on the following conclusions:

1) Would enable the GPO to perform an important statutory requirement that has been delayed for several years— a service for the 1200 Congressionally-designated Depository Libraries, and the public in every state that needs and desires the information contained in government publications.

2) Would cost at least $1.7 million less annually than printing and distributing non-GPO documents in hard copy.

3) The potential saving in terms of dollars and space on "GPO-documentation" is indicated by a pilot project on conversion of the Code of Federal Regulations (CFR). . . .

In print form, the CFR ran to 137 hefty volumes and weighed 168 pounds. In microfiche form that entire CFR weighed only a total of 14 pounds 8 ounces. The cost of mailing alone was 76% less for the microfiche CFR than for the printed books.

4) As to "non-GPO-documentation"—A GPO study conducted for JCP found that the cost of printing hard-copies of the estimated 6000 titles required by the depositories would be $1,950,000 whereas the filming and conversion to microfiche of that same material would total $403,920 . . . and the savings in postal costs, alone, would be $216,000 the first year. Additional sizable savings also are foreseen in terms of library space, storage, handling ease, etc.[10]

As a result, a growing number of GPO documents will become available on microfiche, inevitably increasing awareness of microforms and, eventually, achieving more ready acceptance on the part of researchers.

Of great significance in the development of micropublishing were the extensive programs undertaken by the Library of Congress and the National Archives. The Library of Congress began filming selections from its own holdings in 1948 with the aid of a grant from the Rockefeller Foundation. Today, it is the largest single source of photoreproductions for scholarly purposes in the United States. Its microform program includes (1) preparation of single copies for individuals, scholars, and libraries; (2) microfilming of research materials as master copies for micropublishers; and (3) microfilming archives and other forms of documentation that require preservation. Many of these collections, not attractive as commercial ventures, are filmed by the Library of Congress solely for preservation purposes and to assist scholars by making possible the dissemination of research materials that otherwise would be difficult to obtain.

The National Archives also received a Rockefeller Brothers Foundation grant in 1948 that enabled it to undertake its own microfilming program.[11] It concentrates on documents and records of "high research value" and as of 1974 had produced more than 100,000 reels of master microfilm from which copies had been sold or distributed to various national depositories.[12]

When microform usage first began to expand in the 1940s, it had become apparent that standards would be required to provide some degree of uniformity. Three British librarians were among the first authorities in the field to recognize and address this problem:

> Microphotography promises to supply the librarian with the solution of some of his most difficult problems, but the fulfillment of this promise can only be attained if from the outset we avoid a confusing diversity of sizes and types of microcopies. The subject is young, and if we now adopt a policy of rigid standardization, we are likely to save ourselves much recrimination in the future.[13]

In the United States in 1943, the National Bureau of Standards established standards for both temporary and permanent record photographic microcopying film. Four years later, in 1947, the Association of Research Libraries[14] in conjunction with the newly established National Microfilm Association agreed upon an industry standard for newspaper microfilming. Next, in 1954, the American Library Association published the *Guide to Microfilming Practices,* soon followed by the Library of Congress' guideline, *Specifications for Library of Congress Microfilming.*[15] *Microfilm Norms* (1966), an American Library Association publication, established standards for the micropublishing of scholarly materials. At this point, while differences in approach among the various guidelines remained,[16] scholarly micropublishing had achieved a certain degree of uniformity and quality. Today, the industry adheres to the standards set by the American National Standards Institute (ANSI), formerly the National Bureau of Standards. The institute is a nongovernmental association of users and manufacturers. Its PH 5 committee is responsible for matters related to the photographic reproduction documents.

In addition to the adoption of standards, a number of technological developments bolstered the growth of micropublishing in the postwar years. Of these, perhaps the most dramatic was the introduction of the Xerox copyflo machine in 1956. It enabled micropublishers to produce paper books economically in editions of one copy. The copyflo makes paper prints as microfilm passes through it. There is very little waste between each exposure, and electrically controlled automatic cutters separate each page or camera exposure from 1,500 to 2,000 foot lengths of 11-inch wide paper. The continuity of the process and the length of the paper make the copyflo an extremely economical means of reproduction.[17]

The first micropublisher to adopt the copyflo process was Eugene Power who used it to reproduce in hard copy back files of dissertations, as well as new titles. Costs were minimal—only 3½ cents per page. (The dissertations were bound in soft cover.) Power was also able to launch a new O-P (out-of-print) book program which he described as a by-product of micropublishing:

The Xerox service of University Microfilms, Inc. is based on the same economies as the making of positive microfilm: it is a straightline cost process, the cost per unit remaining constant, once the negative film has been made, whether 1, 10 or 100 copies are produced. In this process the final product of the microfilm negative is a life-size paper copy rather than a microcopy on film or photographic paper. The image can be laid on any kind of paper, it is permanent, and, if the microfilm negative is good, it is clear and sharp. A satisfactory type of flexible glued binding has been developed to make a book from the loose Xerox sheets.

With the technological problems solved, the realization of Binkley's dream of publication upon demand becomes a practical reality for paper copies as well as for the positive microfilm. Though microfilm has many broad applications, there are uses for which the full size paper copy is more desirable. Microfilm positives are especially indicated for the preservation of newspapers, and for little-used periodical files, where space saving and ease of handling are primary considerations. The economies of the microfilm negative make it an ideal medium for copying and storing a variety of other kinds of library materials. The many types of reproductions which originate with microfilm negative combine to make it an ideal master medium for the preservation of recorded information, later to be reproduced as microfilm positive, Xerox prints, or offset plates, depending on the need.[18]

In addition to the out-of-print books program undertaken by University Microfilms, the copyflo technique lent itself to other uses. These included (1) duplication of rare books and manuscripts without fear of damaging a valuable original; (2) replacement in usable form of important books that were deteriorating; (3) publication of original manuscripts in book form with the microfilm negative the only investment cost; (4) conversion to paper copies, at a reasonable cost, of publications that had previously been microfilmed. Furthermore, the technique assured that books need never go out of print.[19]

By using copyflo, it was possible to duplicate manuscripts handwritten in monasteries, the limited editions of early printers, and the larger editions of modern printers. Publishers were now able to produce smaller editions via the offset process and to obtain, on microfilm, single copies of out-of-print books.[20]

Another technological development that has great potential for both library management and scholarly research is the combination of computer technology with micropublishing. This merging of the speed of the computer and the reduction capacities of microphotography has made possible the creation of data bases—the computerization of bodies of information—for both bibliographic and book cataloging purposes.

Computer output microfilm (COM) recorders which convert the computer's electronic signals to readable characters on microfilm were introduced in 1956. The most up-to-date COM recorders now available can imprint up to 50,000 lines of text per minute directly on microfilm. Thus, depending on the reduction ratio, the equivalent of a good-sized library's card catalog (about 250,000 items) can be stored on a single reel of microfilm with space left over.[21] These COM catalogs can be readily duplicated and updated and are less expensive to maintain than book catalogs.

COM's reference book application is of particular value to scholars. Although reference works constitute some 20 percent of trade book sales in the United States each year, because of the nature of book publishing, their contents are often dated by the time they appear.[22] There rarely is such a thing as a current reference book.

The following hypothetical situation envisions how COM could be used for continuous updating of reference books:

> The reference book buyer would receive upon publication a traditionally published book containing all the data gathered by the book's editors up to the cutoff date required for the traditional printing-publishing process. In addition, inserted in pockets in the back of the book would be COM-generated microfiche containing all the cumulated information gathered by the book's editors from the initial cutoff to a supplemental cutoff date as little as a week before actual shipment of the newly published book.

> The publisher's reference work need not be current simply upon publication. Subsequent cumulated microfiche updates can be produced on a monthly basis from the continuing editing the publisher's staff must do to prepare the subsequent edition. . . . A current updating technique could extend the useful life of many reference books by years and lower the level of risk in publishing large production runs of expensive printed books.[23]

COM was first used in this way in 1978 when Whitaker's, a leading British reference book publisher, undertook to update its *British Books in Print* on a monthly basis with COM microfiche.[24]

The Whitaker decision is certain to be regarded as a benchmark in reference book publishing history.

Technological improvement has also made possible the use of microforms to provide "on demand" publication of monographs, one of University Microfilms' newest programs. From camera ready copies of books provided by other publishers, the firm produces paper copies that are bound and sold at a cost of approximately 6 to 6½ cents per page. The book's original publisher provides an abstract of about 300 words to be used for promotional purposes and pays a publication fee to cover promotional costs. University Microfilms creates a master microfiche from the camera ready copy. To produce the monograph, it utilizes a Xerox Model 970 copier capable of producing up to 3,300 pages per hour from negative microfiche and collating sets at about 2 cents per page plus the cost of labor. University Microfilms promotes the book via mailing lists supplied by the publisher and in its own journal *Monograph Abstracts*. It also handles shipping and invoicing. The imprint of the original publisher appears on the book, but although the book is listed in the original publisher's catalog, University Microfilms retains exclusive distribution rights. Royalty payments generally are 10 percent of net cash receipts.

The Monograph Publishing Program may also be used by individuals who want to assure that works which otherwise might be rejected by publishers are "in print."[25]

Despite the progress that helped micropublishers better serve the more esoteric needs of scholars, the industry owes a great deal to the dramatic expansion of the academic market in the United States in the late 1950s and early 1960s. The launch of the Soviet satellite Sputnik (October 4, 1957) was a profound shock to the United States. It inspired passage by Congress of far-reaching legislation designed to upgrade American education—the National Defense Education Act and the Library Service Act (the first legislation authorizing federal funding for libraries).[26] As a result, educational enrollments from 1958 to 1968 alone equaled the growth of the previous 300 years.[27] To accommodate the needs of this larger student population, new libraries had to be built and stocked with books. This sparked the development of the scholarly reprint industry. Reprint publishing made possible the sale of new copies of scholarly works that were available at some earlier date from another publisher or institution. Reprints are generally (but not exclusively) produced by a photographic process and are intended to satisfy a relatively small, specialized market.

Federal support for education continued to expand in the 1960s. According to the National Center for Educational Statistics, during that decade "federal contributions to higher education followed a steadily rising pattern. By the end of 1969 (sparked by the Great Society Program of the Johnson Administration) federal funds accounted for more than one-fifth of the total budget of the nation's colleges, universities and professional schools."[28] During the same period, the number of libraries in the United States increased from 15,860 to 29,163 (not counting school libraries). At the college and university level, 515 libraries were established, increasing the total number from 1,379 in 1960 to 1,896 by the end of the decade. More than 400 new two-year and community colleges were established, raising the number of these institutions from 645 in 1960 to 1,072 at the end of 1969.

This rapid educational growth helped spark the concept of the packaged library which, in turn, led to the suggestion, in 1962, that microforms containing books might eventually be dispensed from vending machines:

> From all indications, we now have the technical capability of distributing low-cost, expendable microform copies of books (by vending machine or manually). It is probably possible to produce micro-transparencies or micro-opaques that could be sold at a cost of ten cents. Let us project the possibilities inherent in these potentialities, in symbiotic combination. This might introduce a complete new dimension in the mass distribution of knowledge, comparable to the mass market paperback or the LP record.[29]

Another dramatic illustration of the "packaged library" concept was contained in a 1968 Rand Corporation report, *A Billion Books for Education in America and the World*.[30] It envisioned ultrafiche, enabling assemblage of 1,000 libraries with 1 million books each. That same year the Encyclopaedia Britannica established a subsidiary, Library Resources, Inc., to create ultrafiche libraries.[31] Its "package" was based on the "microbook" and derived from a total systems approach to utilizing microforms. This system approach was described as follows by a noted micrographics consultant:

> It was to be designed with the express purpose of serving library needs more economically and more efficiently than any previous library microform. The fact that the form would be different was dictated by analysis of the system requirements and a commitment to realize these requirements in an integrated system. Because no existing microform was capable of meeting the system requirements, a new microform had to be devised. The final form was a microfiche comparatively small in size, but having a much greater capacity than conventional microfiche.[32]

The first package published by Library Resources was *The Library of American Civilization* (LAC), advertised as containing "6,000,000 pages, approximately 20,000 volumes and over 12,000 titles."[33] According to the publisher, the content of the collection was limited to "American Civilization, Beginnings to 1914." The fiches were designed to fit existing library filing equipment, and on the front of the envelope containing them was a facsimile of a full catalog card envelope providing complete bibliographic information. Because of the 1,000-page capacity of the ultrafiche, one fiche could contain one complete book. A second "trailer" fiche was required only for the occasional book of more than 1,000 pages.

LAC was criticized both for its new format (ultrafiche)[34] and for its many out-of-date titles. However, the concept or systems approach was praised. As one critic phrased it:

> *[The Library of American Civilization]* . . . was not the first publication of library materials at high reduction. Nor is it significant merely because it demonstrated for the first time an alternative high reduction technology fully developed for mass production. It has, however, become a milestone because of its total systems design.[35]

Despite increasing federal support for education in the 1960s and 1970s, private foundations continued the tradition established by early grants from the Carnegie and Rockefeller foundations in furthering the growth of micropublishing. However, the greatest source of private support became the Council on Library Resources (CLR), founded in 1956 and funded with a $5 million Ford Foundation grant.[36] CLR was created

> for the purpose of aiding in the solution of the problems of libraries generally and research libraries in particular, conducting research in, developing and demonstrating new techniques and methods, and disseminating through any medium the results thereof, and for making grants to other institutions and persons for such purposes; and for providing leadership, and wherever appropriate, coordination of efforts (1) to develop the resources and services of libraries and (2) to improve relations between American and foreign libraries and archives.[37]

In its second annual report, the CLR announced its intention of entering micrographics, stating succinctly that "it (microfilm) has created perhaps fully as many problems as it has solved."[38] Approximately 40 percent of CLR's funds for its first two years were expended on micrographics and preservation research.[39] One of its projects was an attempt to develop an inexpensive, hand-held viewing device "that would allow readers to use microfilm almost as easily and pleasurably as books!"[40] It also explored methods by which research materials could be more widely disseminated. One notable result of this effort was publication of the first scholarly periodical in microfilm, *Wildlife Disease,* the forerunner of several scholarly journals now published exclusively in microform.[41]

While these developments so vital to the growth of scholarly micropublishing in the United States were taking place, in Europe and Great Britain progress was much slower. Two major factors were responsible—a tradition of user resistance to microforms and the disruption of World War II. A few countries made notable progress, however.

The first modern French micropublishing organization was established in 1948 by William Hawkins, a Frenchman of English descent who had served in the American Army V Mail section. The bulk of his work, however, was in records-keeping.[42] Micropublishing made greater headway in the Netherlands where Dr. L. J. van der Wolk of the Delft Technology University and Dr. Joseph Goebel, the German developer of the microfiche, formed an association to explore the possible uses of this new medium. Their work culminated in the formation of the Mickrokaart Stichting (Microcard Foundation). The name was anglicized in 1954 because, as van der Wolk put it:

> . . . the word microfiche as an internationally accepted word did not exist. At this time we only knew of the microcard, which could be opaque or transparent. . . . When, however, a similar thing, but transparent, as film sheet came into being the advantages were obvious. Easier reproduction, better image, smaller, so cheaper [sic] reading apparatus so on . . . we may truly call Dr. J. Goebel of Mainz the inventor, the father of the transparent microcard. But then . . . Mr. H. R. Verry, the photographic expert of the British Museum, objected to this word. A card in English cannot be transparent, that is a contradiction in terms. He then suggested borrowing the French word microfiche and to pronounce it the English way. We were only too happy to have hit upon this international-spirited solution and from that day on we speak of a *microcard* as an opaque flat microfilm, and a *microfiche* as a transparent flat microform. And that is why the Mickrokaart Stichting now in the international world is the Microfiche Foundation.[43]

In Sweden, one of van der Wolk's former students, Henri deMink, pursued his own interest in microfiche as a means of disseminating information. Although employed as an engineer, he used his free time to visit several European national libraries as well as UNESCO headquarters seeking support for a cooperative venture to develop a union list of micropublished materials. Receiving no encouragement, deMink began to compile his own list which eventually was published in the newspaper *Micro-Library*. By the time five issues of this English language publication had appeared, he was determined to enter micropublishing himself.

DeMink's decision resulted from his frustration in dealing with a Swedish newsclipping service in Lund. He had been forced to wait to borrow clippings until another individual had finished using them. The incident led to his idea for microfiche editions of clippings. When librarians at several Swedish institutions expressed interest,[44] he moved back to Holland and established Inter Documentation Company. Today, deMink's firm offers monographs, archives, periodicals, newspapers, and other documentation in eighteen subject areas. With nearly 40,000 individual titles in microfiche, Inter Documentation Company has the world's largest list of microfiche publications.[45]

In both Europe and the United States, increasing amounts of scholarly materials are being published in microform. These include several scholarly journals which have followed the lead of *Wildlife Disease* and now appear on fiche in preference to hard copy. Among them are the *International Microform Journal of Legal Medicine*, the *American Journal of Computational Linguistics*, and *Sociology Micro-Journal*.

An even more specialized use has been devised by the Chemical Society (England) and the University of Chicago Press, both of which have experimented with publishing abstracts of articles in microform. More recently, the American Chemical Society has been making available "supplementary material" to its other publishing programs upon request of researchers.[46] Thus, a scientist with more than general interest in a particular area of study could gain access to information otherwise unavailable.[47] As described by an editor of the American Chemical Society, "it is material relevant to the published paper, but which supplies extreme details and/or data."[48]

The advantages of the program are that information can be provided to the scientific community that does not warrant the additional space it would occupy in the printed journal. However, according to its program editor there are some disadvantages: "The main disadvantage is the problem of reeducating the authors, editors, and subscribers. We must get authors to generate acceptable original documents. We must train editors not to accept reams of meaningless paper, simply because it will not be typeset.''[49] Increased acceptance of microforms should make greater amounts of supplementary information available in this manner to those who need it most.

Still another application of microforms is the inclusion with books of microfiche containing charts, tables, maps, and other materials that are difficult to typeset. This "hybrid publication,"[50] as one university press officer calls it, is a book with an envelope for the microfiche inside the back cover. Readers thus would receive the benefits of illustrations and other graphic material that might otherwise be too difficult or too costly to offer.

The use of microfiche publications accompanied by printed texts has been explored for some time as an alternative to presentation of these collections in book form. The National Historical Publications Commission (NHPC) has funded a number of historical and library projects leading to publication of the collected papers of various historical figures on microfilm.[51]

Spiraling production costs have made publication of these collections in book form uneconomical. The cost of producing 1,500 sets of a ten-volume collection can range from $170,000 to $185,000, exclusive of editorial, promotion, and distribution expenses, which can add up to $50,000 more.[52] In addition, these projects are time consuming, requiring a number of years from start to finish.

The first collection to appear in microform was *The Papers of Benjamin Latrobe*,[53] published on microfiche with an accompanying printed edition of related materials. The rationale for adopting this combined format was presented as follows:

> The microfiche edition of *The Papers of Benjamin Henry Latrobe* is designed to serve two purposes. First, it will make the complete collection of Latrobe's works available to librarians and individual researchers in a convenient format, at an affordable cost, and within a reasonably short period of time. Second, it will enable us to publish a selec-

tive, rather than a comprehensive, printed edition. Because a complete record of Latrobe's life will be available in microform, we shall not feel obliged to publish in our printed edition every item that survives from the architect's hand. Routine pieces of correspondence and drawings with few details and no explanatory notes, for example, will be excluded from the printed edition, as will much other peripheral material. Scholars wishing to examine the complete corpus of Latrobe's works, however, will be able to turn to the microfiche edition at least a year before even the first printed volume becomes available.[54]

The complete package consisting of 315 microfiche and a printed index is contained in two binders housed in a box resembling a two-volume reference work. Increasing production costs will force more and more scholarly publishers to adopt this "hybrid" format in order to offer works that might otherwise not be economical to publish.

Unfortunately, the response to microforms as an alternate, economical publishing format continues to be unfavorable. There is no question that the growth of micropublishing has generated a great deal of opposition, particularly in the academic community. While not typical, the following protest does convey some of the irked response microforms provoke:

The first annoyance is, of course, that you cannot take the microfilm home to read in peace, away from students; away from administrators. Either you must closet yourself in the dark, or with greater readiness, but also some discomfort, read down a microscope. The paper is 150 pages long and after ten minutes reading you want to see precisely to what "Blankinsop 1938" refers. So you wind madly to the end, look at the reference and wind back again, finding your place once more with some difficulty. In another ten minutes you wish to refer to a text figure and of course, it is white on black. That is not so bad with a simple line sketch, but with certain types of drawing, histological drawing in particular, white on black conveys nothing, so you moan

and press on regardless. . . . It is often argued that microfilm is so convenient for storage. But as a user I am interested not in the quartermaster aspect of the weapon, but how
it performs in action. By this criterion, microform is a costly
failure. . . . You will see from this why microfilm is a
misery.[55]

Despite the fact that microforms are often the only means of
access to information, there is no question that people do not like
to use them. Aside from the inconvenience they impose, there
are several reasons for this resistance. One of the major problems is that of bibliographic control. Librarians have long been
troubled by this external or cataloging aspect. Since the majority
of micropublications are not cataloged, users often are unaware
that the research material they contain is available in the library.
Thus, they must be cataloged if they are not to be underused, for
as one librarian concluded, "the publication of numerous monographs in microform is not a service to scholarship if the buying
library cannot economically inform its users of the fact."[56]
    A related problem, that of microform indexing, is summarized
as follows:

Perhaps the greatest weakness of current and past microtext
publications has been their lack of adequate bibliographic
control. Librarians have the right to expect that the elementary canons of bibliography which govern ordinary book
publishing should also be applied to microtext publication.
No book publisher would think of trying to publish without
a competent editorial staff. . . . As a result we have reels of
film containing disparate items lacking a table of contents
or even an elementary title page. We have reels of film of
related material with nothing to show on any reel that it
belongs to a larger publication or where it belongs in sequence of the whole publication.[57]

However, the primary reason for user resistance is the inconvenience of working with microforms. Once the page is projected
on the screen, difficulties arise: the reader cannot readily com-

pare several pages, annotate pages, consult the index, or refer
back and forth within the document under study.[58] There is the
further inconvenience of the reading equipment which requires
loading roll film, a difficult process for many users. One librarian
has observed that "most users, patrons and librarians alike,
found the loading method utterly baffling and all too often ended
up with images that were upside down, backwards, or even
worse, confronted with film that refused to wind or unwind.
Worse, improper loading could damage the film severely on
some readers."[59] Another librarian addressing the same subject
offered that "it seems a little surprising that roll film even survived in library usage."[60]

Noise and problems in manipulation and illumination are other
common complaints that underlie user resistance, and there
is the added confusion caused by the variety of microforms in
use.[61] Besides having to evaluate the need for the microform itself, potential purchasers and users alike must consider the fact
that different equipment is needed to read the varied types of
microforms and to produce paper copies if required.

Ultimately, user resistance will be overcome as technological
developments surmount present-day inconveniences, for in the
forty years since Eugene Power formed University Microfilms,
scholarly micropublications have greatly expanded the body of
information accessible to researchers. They have made possible
the preservation of newspaper archives and have vastly reduced
the amount of space required to store them. They have made
available to scholars in their own offices and libraries the contents of otherwise inacessible archives and documents. Computer
output microfilm has facilitated speedier access to information,
and microforms have given out-of-print resources a new lease on
life. Furthermore, it appears that in the not too distant future
some monographs that otherwise would not be published at all
will become available in microform. But problems remain, for as
one observer has noted, "we have in microform publication a
technique of inestimable value, but one whose full potential can
be realized only by the inspiration of rigid standards of selection
and technical performance."[62]

NOTES

1. *Microform Market Place 1980–81* (Westport, Conn.: Microform Review, Inc., 1980), pp. 3–100. The definition of a micropublisher, according to *Microform Market Place 1980–1981*, is based on an organization, either commercial or noncommercial, "that markets micropublished information. Parts catalog micropublishers or publishers of newspapers and periodicals whose respective publications are sold in microform by another organization (e.g. *Time* magazine) are not included."

2. Book sales to libraries for the period 1976–1977 were nearly ten times larger. John D. Dessauer, "Library Acquisitions: A Look into the Future," *Publishers Weekly* 207 (June 16, 1975): 55.

3. Alex Baptie Papers, Naples, Fla.

4. R. R. Dickinson, "The Scholar and the Future of Microfilm," *American Documentation* 17 (1966): 178.

5. The National Aeronautics and Space Administration and the Department of Defense also decided to place their reports on microfiche at about the same time.

6. Interview with Alex Baptie, November 17, 1976.

7. Ian Montagnes, "Microfiche and the Scholarly Publisher," *Scholarly Publishing* 5 (1975): 75.

8. Non-GPO documentation is material printed by government agencies throughout the world in very limited numbers. Though done in authorized government plants, it is printed outside of GPO control. Consequently, it is impossible to predetermine the necessary quantity to fill depository library needs. On the other hand, to film the material and distribute it as microfiche is relatively easy and inexpensive. This type of material includes handbooks, manuals, reports of grant-supported research, agency staff research and study reports, symposiums, advisory group meeting reports and periodicals. Memorandum of Staff Director to Chairman Cannon, March 25, 1977.

9. GPO-documentation includes most major government publications, ranging from the *Congressional Directory* and the *Congressional Record* to the annual reports of the departments and agencies is presently sent to the depository in print format because production is controlled by GPO Documentation. Memorandum of Staff Director to Chairman Cannon, March 25, 1977.

10. Memorandum of Staff Director to Chairman Cannon, March 25, 1977.

11. Papers of the Rockefeller Foundation, Tarrytown, N.Y., Series 200, Box 252, Folder 3016.

12. *National Archives Microfilm Publications,* Catalog 1974.

13. B. S. Page, L. S. Sayre, and E. F. Patterson, "Microphotography: Standards in Format, Storage, and Cataloguing," *The Library Association Record* 40 (1938): 213.

14. The association's work was carried out through its Committee on Microfilming Cooperation. The committee helped in establishing an information center in the Union Catalog Division of the Library of Congress, which in turn led to the publication of *Newspapers on Microfilm: A Union Checklist (1948).* This title is updated periodically by the Library of Congress.

15. The Library of Congress subsequently published specifications for books, newspapers, maps, and manuscripts.

16. The Library of Congress' *Specifications* deals with the preparation of material, targeting, image placement, reduction ratio, film inspection, resolution, packaging, processing, and many miscellaneous matters such as splicing and storage of films. *Norms* covers basically the same areas. There are philosophical differences between *Norms* and *Specifications.* One expert in the field has said that *"Norms* is precriptive and synthetic, while the *Specifications* is empirical and pragmatic."* The use of these guidebooks will yield quality microforms for library and research use. For the best discussion of standards, see Allen B. Veaner, "Microreproduction and Micropublication Technical Standards: What They Mean to You the User," *Microform Review* 3 (1974): 80–85.

17. Donald C. Holmes, "Electrostatic Photoreproduction at the United States Library of Congress," *UNESCO Library Bulletin* 18 (1961): 6. The impetus for producing the copyflo dry enlarger came from the U.S. Navy. The Navy contracted with the Haloid Corporation (the former name of the Xerox Corporation) to produce such a machine for its administrative needs. This is another example of how scholarly micropublishing benefited from industrial and governmental uses of microphotography.

18. Eugene Power, "O-P Books: A Library Breakthrough," *American Documentation* 9 (1958): 273.

19. Ibid., p. 275.

20. Ibid.

21. *20th Annual Report of the Council on Library Resources, Inc.* (Washington, D.C.: Council on Library Resources, Inc., 1976), p. 43.

22. Brett Butler, "Updating the Reference Book Through Microform Supplements," *Microform Review* 3 (1974): 30.

23. Ibid., p. 31.

24. Interview with Wilf Deakin, head of research and development for Whitaker's, June 2, 1977. Subscribers to *British Books in Print* on COM fiche receive new editions each month; a printed version is published annually in December.

25. Montagnes, "Microfiche and the Scholarly Publisher," p. 77.

26. Dessauer, "Library Acquisitions," p. 59.

27. Carol Nemeyer, *Scholarly Reprint Publishing in the United States* (New York: R. R. Bowker Co., 1971), p. 53.

28. Ibid.

29. Robert T. Jordan, "The 'Complete Package' College Library," *College & Research Libraries* 23 (1962): 405.

30. David G. Hays, *A Billion Books for Education in America and the World: A Proposal* (Santa Monica, Calif.: Rand Corp., 1968), p. 79.

31. The NCR Corporation announced a similar venture in the same year, the Photochromic Micro Image System (PCMI) Library Collections.

32. William Hawken, "Systems Instead of Standards," *Library Journal* 98 (1973): 2519.

33. *Library of American Civilization* brochure from Library Resources, Inc., ca. 1971. An analysis by the staff of the George Washington University Library for the National Home Library Foundation of Washington, D.C., found only 9,620 titles and 15,347 volumes. For additional information, see Paul A. Napier, Annette D. Steiner, and Rupert C. Woodward, "The Library Resources Inc., *Library of American Civilization* Demonstration at the George Washington University Library," *Microform Review* 3 (1974): 153–57.

The original list of titles was selected by LAC's editorial staff and submitted to three boards of advisors (scholars from various American universities). Because of copyright considerations, the selected titles had copyrights from 1914 and earlier. For the most thorough analysis of LAC and PCMI, see E. M. Grieder, "Ultrafiche Libraries: A Librarian's View," *Microform Review* 1 (1972): 85–100.

34. This microformat has achieved its greatest success in the automotive parts catalog business.

35. Francis F. Spreitzer, "Developments in Copying, Micrographics, and Graphic Communications, 1971," *Library Resources and Technical Services* 15 (1972): 135–54.

36. *20th Annual Report*, p. 10.

37. Ibid.

38. Ibid., p. 37.

39. Ibid., p. 14.

40. This device was not developed. However, research that went into the project was made available to equipment companies.

41. *20th Annual Report*, p. 15.

42. Hawkins was employed by Herman Fussler of the University of Chicago Library in the late 1930s. He learned about microphotography at the University of Chicago. Interview with William Hawkins, February 20, 1977.

43. Papers of the Microfiche Foundation, Delft Technological University Library, Delft, Holland.

44. Mary E. Hickey, "Inter Documentation Company: A History," *Microform Review* 3 (1974): 108.

45. Interview with Henri deMink, October 8, 1977.

46. Montagnes, "Microfiche and the Scholarly Publisher," p. 77.

47. Marjorie A. Laflin, "Micropublishing Potential in Professional Journal Publications," *Journal of Micrographics* 10 (1977): 281.

48. Ibid.

49. Ibid.

50. Montagnes, "Microfiche and the Scholarly Publisher," p. 77.

51. In 1974, Public Law 93–536 authorized funding that permits the commission to begin assisting state and local organizations in the preservation, arrangement, and description of historical records. To date, 110 personal paper projects have been completed; an additional 29 are at various stages of completion. For additional information, see "Publications Catalog 1976" of the National Historical Publications and Records Commission, pp. 38–87.

52. Eric H. Boehm, "Current Emphasis in the Dissemination of Information about Manuscripts," paper presented at the Conference on the Publication of American Historical Manuscripts, University of Iowa, March 13, 1975, pp. 8–9. A revised paper appears in *The Publication of American Historical Manuscripts*, Leslie W. Dunlap and Fred Shelley, eds. (Iowa City, Iowa, 1976), pp. 57–68.

53. Latrobe (1764–1820) is best known as America's first professional architect and engineer. He did extensive work on the U.S. Capitol.

54. Thomas E. Jeffrey, "The Papers of Benjamin Latrobe: New Approaches to the Micropublication of Historical Records," *Microform Review* 6 (1977): 83.

55. D. W. Ewer, "A Biologist's Reflections on Libraries and Library Service," *South African Libraries* 29 (October 1961): 53–56, 74.

56. Stephen Salmon, "User Resistance to Microforms in the Research

Library," *Microform Review* 3 (1974): 105.

57. John A. Riggs, "The State of Microtext Publications," *Library Trends* 8 (1960): 376.

58. Allen B. Veaner, ed., *Studies in Micropublishing* (Westport, Conn.: Microform Review, 1977), p. 474.

59. Ibid.

60. Salmon, "User Resistance to Microforms," p. 196.

61. The following microforms are available: microfiche; microfilm; micro-opaques (microcards and microtext); ultrafiche; and aperture cards. Roll microfilm may be 16 mm or 35 mm; it may be in cartridges or on conventional reels. Furthermore, microfiche or microfilm may be silver halide, diazo, or vesicular. An excellent explanation of these microforms and their characteristics can be found in Allen B. Veaner, *The Evaluation of Micropublications: A Handbook for Librarians* (Chicago: American Library Association, 1971).

62. Riggs, "State of Microtext Publications," p. 379.

5

SCHOLARLY
MICROPUBLISHING TODAY:
AN OVERVIEW

In their attempt to broaden their own market and meet the needs of scholars and libraries, micropublishers have taken an imaginative and creative approach to vast quantities of research materials. Their task has been not only to provide quality copies in microform but also to make the information contained in those copies readily accessible to the user. This chapter provides an overview of how micropublishing has responded to the sometimes conflicting demands for materials that are exhaustive and comprehensive but are also easily accessible to the scholar.

This demand for scholarly microforms comes, of course, from libraries—academic and public institutions, as well as some 9,000 special libraries maintained by business, government, the legal profession, the armed forces, technical facilities, and museums. In addition to these 9,000 libraries and the 3,900 college, university, and junior/community college libraries in the United States, there are 4,500 libraries in Canada and elsewhere in the world that fit one of the three classifications. However, only a small percentage are large purchasers of scholarly micropublications.

Although it is difficult to estimate the precise number of libraries that have acquired microform materials, it is safe to assume that the several hundred large research institutions throughout the world are potential customers for even the most specialized micropublication. The following table illustrates the growth of microform purchases in college, university, public, and special libraries in the United States for the years 1972 to 1978.[1]

INSTITUTION	1972-1973	1978-1979	CHANGE 1979 FROM 1973
	Millions		Pct.
College and University Libraries	$19.3	$30.5	58.0
Public Libraries	6.0	10.5	75.0
Special Libraries	11.7	20.3	73.5

The next table illustrates total expenditures and the percentage of the total that is for microform purchases (estimated books, periodicals, audiovisual, microform, binding) by college and university libraries, public libraries, and special libraries for the period 1978–1979.[2]

INSTITUTION	1978-1979	PCT. OF TOTAL FOR MICROFORMS
	Millions	Pct.
College and University Libraries	$490.7	6.9
Public Libraries	310.1	3.3
Special Libraries	285.1	7.1

The continued growth of the micropublishing market is assured by a problem common to all libraries—overcrowded conditions that cannot be alleviated during inflationary times by expanding available storage space. As a result, many libraries will inevitably opt to replace paper copies with microforms as a space-saving measure enabling them to maintain and enlarge their research collections. Furthermore, increasingly microforms will be used in combination with the computer to produce updatable reference services as described in Chapter 4.

Despite its broadening role, micropublishing remains a relatively small industry. There are only 319 scholarly micropublishers worldwide, compared to some 5,000 book publishers in the United States alone.[3] Of the 319 organizations, 211 are in the United States, 47 in Great Britain, 14 in Canada, and 12 in France. The rest are scattered among 10 other countries.

Of the 211 American micropublishers, 108 are commercial firms, 93 are noncommercial (societies, national associations, government agencies), and 10 university presses.[4] Thus, the bulk of the $70 million in U.S. micropublishing sales[5] accrues to approximately 108 firms[6] and can be accounted for largely by micropublications of newspapers, serials (periodicals), government documents, and research collections. Examples of these firms' offerings follow.

Carrollton Press of Arlington, Virginia, is primarily a micropublisher of government documents. Among its current offerings are the *Proceedings of the United States Congress (1789–1975)* which includes the *Congressional Record* and its predecessors; the checklist of *United States Public Documents* (1789–1975) which combines a microfilm copy of the shelf-list of the *Superintendent of Documents' Public Documents Library* with five computer-generated indexes in twenty-one volumes; and the *United States Government Bibliography Masterfile (1924–1973)* which contains the full text of more than 40,000 bibliographies published by the federal government since 1924 and is accompanied by a seven-volume *Cumulative Subject Guide.* The latest offering from Carrollton Press is the *Declassified Documents Reference System* which includes formerly classified documents that have been declassified following specific requests from individuals. Despite their declassification, these documents would undoubtedly have remained inaccessible if not for Carrollton's reference system which searches them out, indexes and abstracts them, and makes them available in microfiche for use by historians and other scholars and researchers.[7]

A relatively new micropublishing firm has specialized in documents relating to the work of the Indian Claims Commission, a body that hears and decides claims made against the federal government in regard to lands ceded by Indians during the "treaty period" of United States-Indian relations. Between its founding in 1972 and the present, the Clearwater Publishing Company of New York City has made available on microfiche more than 370,000 pages of historical, legal, and anthropological materials on the American Indian. Its published collections include the *Decisions of the Indian Claims Commission* (with printed index); the *Expert Testimony Before the Indian Claims Commission* with printed index); the *Transcripts of Oral Testimony before the Indian Claims Commission; Briefs and Exhibit Digests before the Indian Claims Commission,* which include General Accounting Office reports before the commission (with printed index); and the *Legislative History of the Indian Claims Commission Act.*[8]

The leading commercial indexer and micropublisher of current reference materials issued by the federal government is Congressional Information Service (CIS) of Washington, D.C., established in 1969. CIS provides printed bibliographies, indexes, or other finding aids for each of its microform collections. It provides a printed index to its "Microfiche Library" entitled *Index to Publications of the United States Congress.* The "publications of Congress" cover an enormous amount of material; for 1978 alone, the estimate was 875,000 pages in 3,900 titles. Several options are available for acquiring the complete or limited parts of the CIS Microfiche Library, including just the *Serial Set* (congressionally published information) or just the *Hearings.* Earlier volumes of the *Serial Set* are available in total or in part from the *CIS United States Serial Set on Microfiche (1789–1969).* A complete *Serial Set,* with its 14,000 volumes, stretches aisle after aisle and presents an imposing sight to the researcher. Because it lacks adequate indexes, the wealth of information it contains is often inaccessible. The *CIS Serial Set Index* has made the *Serial Set* accessible for the first time through one comprehensive hardbound index. CIS also makes available in microfiche the more than 40,000 bills and resolutions introduced in Congress since 1967.

Another CIS offering is its *American Statistics Index Microfiche Library* with its accompanying *American Statistics Index.* The reference value of this printed index and microfiche collection of more than 900,000 pages of material yearly is incalculable. Each of the tens of thousands of documents in the retrospective and current CIS and ASI Microfiche Libraries is included in a bibliographic data base. Individual microfiche can be identified and ordered on-line, enabling users to read the document on a computer terminal or to cite the document in the printed indexes and order by mail.[9]

Greenwood Press of Westport, Connecticut, offers twenty-eight different research collections as well as government document titles. Seven of these collections are periodicals no longer in print. They include "Black Journals"; "Periodicals on Woman and Women's Rights"; "Radical Periodicals in the United States, 1930–1960"; "Radical Periodicals of Great Britain, 1794–1914"; "Science Fiction Periodicals"; "Social Welfare Periodicals"; and "Agrarian Periodicals in the United States, 1920–1960." Other Greenwood offerings include *Plantation Records* of nineteen families from the Louisiana State University Department of Archives and *Baedeker's Handbooks for Travelers* (266 editions in English between 1861 and 1939). These "handbooks" provide guides to the social, economic, and political histories of thirty-one countries.

Greenwood Press also publishes a number of government documents including the *United States Congressional Committee Prints* (from the first issued through 1969) with clothbound bibliographies, indexes, or shelf-lists; the *United States Congressional Hearings* (from the first issued through 1969), also with clothbound bibliography and indexes; the *Witness Index to the United States Congressional Hearings (1939–1966)*, a microfiche card-file index; *United States Census Reports and Serials* (those that were not included in the decennial census publications issued from 1820 through 1967), with accompanying printed catalogs; and the *National Monetary Commission Publications* (Volumes 1–23, 1909–1911).[10]

Government documents are also available from the Kraus-Thomson Organization (KTO) of Millwood, New York. Kraus-Thomson, which began micropublishing in 1970, offers *Industrial America (1900–1940),* a set that includes publications of the Bureau of Labor, the Securities and Exchange Commission, the Federal Trade Commission, the Bureau of Corporations, and the

Federal Reserve System. Its "American Indian" set includes publications from the Smithsonian Institution, the Bureau of Indian Affairs, and the Department of the Interior.

KTO also publishes on microform a variety of periodicals on business, economics, science, and Judaica, as well as the collected papers of such historical figures as Charles Willson Peale, the noted American artist. Perhaps its most significant micropublication is that of the more than 65,000 volumes and 226,000 manuscripts by and about blacks contained in the Schomburg Center for Research in Black Culture of the New York Public Library.[11]

Still another micropublisher, Lost Cause Press of Louisville, Kentucky, emphasizes collections of books based on published bibliographies. Its best known offering is *Travels in the Confederate States,* based on the bibliography by E. M. Coulter, as well as *Travels in the Old South* and *Travels in the New South,* both based on Thomas D. Clark's bibliographies. Lost Cause has also published *Anti-Slavery Propaganda in the Oberlin College Library,* a collection of American antislavery pamphlets published before 1863.[12]

The Microfilming Corporation of America (MCA) of Sanford, North Carolina, is a division of the New York Times Company. The bulk of its revenues derive from sales of yearly microfilm subscriptions to *The New York Times.* By 1979, the number of subscriptions had reached an unprecedented 4,500,[13] reflecting the *Times'* unofficial status as the "national" newspaper of the United States.

In addition to its newspaper micropublishing program, MCA offers several research collections, including the *New York Times Oral History Program* consisting of eighteen separate collections containing thousands of memoirs. Titles range from the American Film Institute's *Louis B. Mayer Oral History Collection* with memoirs from participants in all aspects of the film industry to *The Modern Congress in American History,* containing memoirs of former members of Congress. The most impressive segment of the oral history program is the *Columbia University Oral History Collection* founded by the late Allan Nevins, a distinguished historian. It includes personal memoirs as well as projects covering subjects such as the occupation of Japan, the development of aviation, and military affairs.[14]

The Micro Photo Division of Bell & Howell, located in Wooster, Ohio, specializes in the microfilm sales of 7,100 small and medium-sized city newspapers in the United States and abroad. Micro Photo also publishes several research collections. The most innovative collection, called *Phonefiche*, offers current telephone directories on microfiche of areas of 25,000 or more population in forty-four states.[15]

Another micropublisher offering both research collections and government documents is Research Publications of Woodbridge, Connecticut. Among the research collections it offers is the *City Directories of the United States, 1786–1901*, which contains hundreds of early directories and provides scholars with data on American life and society that otherwise would be unobtainable. Another collection is the *Goldsmiths'-Kress Library of Economic Literature: Resources in Economic, Social, Business and Political History of Modern Industrial Society.* It merges the holdings of Harvard University's Kress Library with those of the Goldsmiths' Library at the University of London (London School of Economics). The collection encompasses some 30,000 titles, all of which have been indexed. Research Publications has also assembled a collection entitled *American Fiction 1774–1910* based on Lyle H. Wright's bibliography of the same name. The 15,500 titles in the collection include American prose fiction (novels, short stories, romances, tales, travels, sketches, and allegories) published between 1774 and 1910.

Research Publications' microform editions of government documents include a microfilm or microfiche edition of the *Official Gazette of the United Patent Office.* The firm also publishes patents on microfilm in reel or cartridge format with purchase options, including all patents, chemical patents, electrical patents, or general and mechanical patents. It also markets in microfilm more than 380,000 pages of census publications for the years 1790 through 1970, with a printed bibliographic guide which is a research tool in its own right. Still another offering is the microfilm publication of the *Administration Histories of World War II Civilian Agencies of the Federal Government.* This collection includes histories from fifty-seven different agencies, ranging from the American Commission for the Protection and Salvage of Artistic and Historic Monuments in War Areas to the War Refugee Board.[16]

One of the cornerstones of University Microfilms International since its founding in 1938 has been its serials program. Today University Microfilms International lists approximately 12,000 periodical titles that are available on microfilm or microfiche.[17] In addition, University Microfilms International has assembled a number of research collections on microform. These include *Sotheby's Annotated Sales Catalogs, 1734–1970*, a record of sellers and buyers of specific items and the dates of sale. The collection serves as a reference work for bibliographic research, as well as an historic guide to changing interests in art. Another University Microfilms offering is *The Papers of Daniel Webster*, one of many collections of personal papers of notable Americans it has published on microform. The collection consists of 16,000 items written both by and to Daniel Webster from 1798 through 1852. Documents are organized chronologically. An accompanying 175-page *Guide and Index* contains a descriptive, reel-by-reel summary of the papers.[18]

This overview of the offerings of some of the larger micropublishers illustrates the wide range of micropublished research materials now available to scholars. Although no single source lists every micropublication currently available, the *Guide to Microforms in Print 1980* lists nearly 100,000 that have been published.[19]

Clearly, scholarly micropublishing has evolved from an ambitious, though perhaps naive, idea to a thriving industry. It has had to adapt itself to some challenges which its pioneers did not foresee—specifically, the need to go beyond the mechanical task of microphotography to provide products complete with indexing aids. How these publishers have managed and mastered the task of assembling and indexing the vast quantities of research materials they offer is described in the following chapters focusing on three distinctive micropublishing programs.

NOTES

1. John P. Dessauer, "Library Acquisitions: A Look into the Future," *Publishers Weekly* 207 (June 16, 1975): 55.

2. Ibid., p. 56.

3. *Microform Market Place 1980–1981* (Westport, Conn.: Microform Review, Inc., 1980), pp. 3–100. As previously noted in this study, a micropublisher is defined as an organization, either commercial or non-commercial, that markets micropublished information.

4. *Microform Market Place*, pp. 159–64.

5. Dessauer, "Library Acquisitions," p. 56.

6. Approximately 8 percent of these commercial firms account for 90 percent of the sales.

7. Carrollton Press Inc., United States Historical Documents Inc. catalog entitled *1978–79 Publications List.*

8. Clearwater Publishing Company promotion brochure (untitled).

9. Congressional Information Service catalog entitled *CIS 1978–1979 Catalog.*

10. Greenwood Press catalog entitled *1978 Greenwood Microform Catalog.* Greenwood Press was acquired by Congressional Information Service in August 1976. It now operates as an affiliated company.

11. Kraus-Thomson Organization catalog entitled *General Catalog 1978–1979.*

12. Lost Cause Press catalog entitled *Lost Cause Press Microfiche Collections 1977–1978, Volume Five/Number One.*

13. This figure is an estimate based on discussions with the president of MCA, Karl Horwitz, January 4, 1980.

14. Microfilming Corporation of America catalog entitled *1978 Publications.*

15. Micro Photo catalog entitled *1979–1980 Catalog.*

16. Research Publications catalog entitled *1979 Descriptive Catalogue of Microfilm Collections and Bibliographies.*

17. University Microfilms International catalog entitled *Serials in Microform 1979–1980.*

18. University Microfilms International catalog entitled *A Catalog of Research Materials.*

19. Ardis Carleton, ed., *Guide to Microforms in Print 1980* (Westport, Conn.: Microform Review, Inc., 1980). A companion *Subject Guide* is published by the same firm. It lists the 100,000 titles under 138 different subjects.

6

RESEARCH PUBLICATIONS'
LEAGUE OF NATIONS
DOCUMENTS COLLECTION

As Robert Binkley emphasized so long ago,[1] micropublishing can vastly increase access to a wide range of research materials that otherwise would remain beyond the reach of most scholars. Previous chapters have mentioned some of the more notable collections available on microform today. This chapter goes beyond verification of the fact that valuable research collections are now offered on microform to analyze in depth the process of locating, identifying, and indexing a collection of historical documents. It is presented as a case study in order to illustrate the scope of the modern micropublisher's task, particularly as it pertains to the creation of an index or finding aid designed to provide scholars with the ready access so vital to their work.

The collection chosen for this case study is the *League of Nations Documents Collection* published in 1973 by Research Publications, Inc., of Woodbridge, Connecticut. The company's founder, Samuel Freedman, sold his first micropublishing company, Micro Photo (discussed in Chapter 3), to Bell & Howell in 1962. Four years later, in 1966, he established Research Publications, Inc., for the express purpose of micropublishing significant archives and documents.

At the time, the League of Nations itself was no more than a historical memory. It had been dissolved in 1946 to be replaced the following year by the United Nations. With headquarters in Geneva, Switzerland, the League had been composed of an

Assembly in which every member had one vote, a nine-member Council with the five great powers as permanent members and four rotating members, and a Court of International Justice at the Hague, the Netherlands. During the twenty-five years of its existence, the League had published thousands of documents. A number had been formally published, and others had been printed in the League's *Official Journal* or other relevant serials. However, the sale and distribution of the documents was uneven as Catharine J. Reynolds noted in a 1973 *Microform Review* article:

> During the years of its existence, the League of Nations had a world-wide depository system. It sold most of its publications, but although some titles became best sellers, at no time were there more than 156 comprehensive subscriptions to the total sales output. Official libraries had the most complete collections, but confidential documents were circulated only to members, and some were not published other than in the original mimeographed edition.[2]

The problem of assembling a complete collection was not limited to libraries. Indeed, by 1947 although an impressive mass of League documents and publications reposed in the Archives of the League of Nations at Geneva and at the United Nations Library in New York, no single complete set was known to exist.[3]

The bulk of what had been published related to the issues deliberated by the Assembly and Council and classified by the Secretariat under the following subject headings:

Administrative Commissions
Minorities
Financial Section and Economic Intelligence
Service (Financial Questions)
Section of Economic Relations (Economic Questions)
Health
Social Questions

Legal Questions
Mandates
Communications and Transit
Disarmament
Financial Administration of the League of Nations
Traffic in Opium and Other Dangerous Drugs
Intellectual Cooperation
International Bureau
Refugees
General Questions

By far, most of the published documents were those prepared as working papers for use during the deliberations of the Assembly and the Council. Some were in the form of circular letters to member-states. All told, 23,000 documents or document sets fell into the broad category of Assembly, Council, or circular letter documents.

In a second major category were the documents prepared by the various committees and commissions operating under the Secretariat and functioning as its executive arms. These commissions and committees were the primary source of input to the Secretariat for the preparation of Assembly, Council, and circular letter documents. Of the commission documents, some were published independently, and some found their way into the Assembly and the Council in revised or summary forms.[4]

Other League documents included minutes of the early directors' meetings with attached confidential circulars, various smaller series of documents prepared by the Secretariat on matters ranging from housekeeping (turning out the lights in the offices, petty thievery on the premises) to communications received from the outside by the League. These were concerned chiefly with the attitudes of various member- and potential member-states toward the League itself in its early days.[5]

The League also published serials relating to the issues with which it was concerned. The most important of these ranged from health and epidemiological reports to money and banking and the trade in arms, ammunitions, and other implements of war.[6]

Clearly, a decision to publish the League documents in micro-form would represent a formidable commitment. The fact that no complete set was known to exist served as both an impediment and an incentive to undertake the project. From a scholarly point of view, the need was evident: researchers wishing to delve deeply into the role of the League in world history between World War I and II had little choice but to travel to the archives in Geneva to study documents that had never been placed on public sale. Then, too, there was an equally important need for preservation: most of the documents had been printed on very poor quality paper that was rapidly deteriorating.[7]

One of the first to broach the idea of micropublishing the League documents was Joseph Groesbeck, former deputy director of the United Nations Library in New York. He discussed the idea with Samuel Freedman in 1957 when Freedman was still with Micro Photo. Even though he was not prepared to act upon it at the time, Freedman was intrigued with Groesbeck's proposal: "Joe tried to get me and others interested in microfilming the League documents. But it seemed to be such a horrendous job that I shied away from it, and ultimately others did too."[8] However, after he had established Research Publications, Freedman paid a social call on Groesbeck at the United Nations and found that his old friend remained anxious to promote the micropublication of League of Nations documents. Although he still viewed the project with trepidation, Freedman was interested enough to investigate further:

> I discussed it with (the late) John Ottemiller, associate librarian at Yale [University]. He told me that when he had been the State Department librarian, he had tried unsuccessfully to put together a whole set of League documents. He also introduced me to people at the State Department library, but as Ottemiller had said, their set was incomplete.[9]

Indeed, Freedman found that no one seemed to know what constituted a full set. Libraries that had received League publications either by deposit or subscription were for the most part

unaware that their collections were incomplete. To make matters worse, the two most commonly used methods of organizing
them did not particularly lend themselves to preservation or to
access by researchers, as Catharine Reynolds observes in *Microform Review:*

> The most commonly used methods were full cataloguing
> and integration of series and monographs with the regular
> book collection or employing the World Peace Foundation's
> "uniform plan for permanent binding," which consisted of
> binding the publications in groups by sales number, with
> the title and contents sheets supplied by the foundation.
>
> Neither plan fared very well as a means of preserving the
> collection. Those organized by the first method suffered the
> typical fate of small paperbound publications scattered
> throughout a large book collection; sometimes actual physi-
> cal loss, sometimes burial by the vagaries of author entries.
> Collections accorded the second treatment, which at least
> had the merit of keeping documents in one location, be-
> came dog-earred as a result of binding thin, legal-sized
> documents next to fat octavos, since the sales numbers sel-
> dom brought the serials together.[10]

Although the task of assembling a complete set of League of
Nations documents appeared formidable, at Groesbeck's urging
Freedman began to think seriously about undertaking their
micropublication. Accordingly, in 1967 Research Publications
came to a verbal agreement with the United Nations Library to
do some preliminary work in order to determine the scope and
manageability of the project.[11]

There were two major reference works pertaining to the
League documents: the *Key to League of Nations Documents Placed
on Public Sale, 1920–1929* and *Supplements* (Boston and New
York, 1930–1936) by Marie Carroll and *Guide to League of
Nations Publications* (New York, 1966) by Hans Aufrict. In addi-
tion, the League itself had compiled a *Catalogue of Publications
Vol. I, 1920–1935* and *Vol. II, 1935–1946* (Geneva, 1935–1947?).
These tools were limited in that they were restricted to docu-

ments that had been placed on public sale by the League. Research Publications editors working at the United Nations Library in New York were confronted by a mass of documents confirming that (1) none of the library's three sets was a complete one; (2) no one knew what a complete set was; and (3) a great deal of the material—perhaps as much as half—had never been published and offered for sale. Indeed, much of it existed in typescript only.[12]

The editors were unable to determine exactly how many of the Assembly, Council, and circular letter documents they found had never been published in any other form. Reno describes the problem in his introduction to the guide to the documents eventually published in microform by Research Publications, Inc.:

It is impossible to say exactly how many of these Assembly, Council and Circular Letter documents were never published in any other form whatsoever, since this would require tracing the pedigree and successive metamorphoses of the thousands of documents that do exist in mimeographed form. Some rough comparisons are available, however. One notes, for example that Marie Carroll in her *Key to League of Nations Documents Placed on Public Sale* (1920–1929) and *Supplements* (Boston and New York, 1930–1936), lists 13 documents with official numbers as having been placed on public sale by the League for category IB between the years 1919–1934 (IB was the category designation assigned to documents treating Minorities questions). For the entire period for which there are IB documents (i.e., 1919–1940), the microfilm collection contains over 1,400 such documents. Most of these are document sets with many parts. Similarly, for category VII, Political Questions, Carroll lists 94 documents with official numbers for the 1919–1934 period, while for the whole period of 1919–1946 the microfilm collection contains over 4,100 category VII documents. Even for a category such as Health (III), where one would assume there were few questions of confidentiality involved, Carroll lists 75 official number documents for the 1919–1934 period, while the

microfilm collection contains over 400 documents in this
category for the 1919–1946 period.[13]

The staff also found that all the documents had been classified
according to a complex numbering system. Each number consisted of a letter prefix indicating its source. The letter "A," for
instance, meant that the document in question was distributed to
the Assembly; "C" indicated the Council; "CL," a circular letter
from the Secretariat; and "H" that the document was directed to
all Member-States. Another part of the identifier was a sequence
number that merely indicated that the document was the first,
third, or twelfth distributed to that particular arm of the League
during the year indicated, which is the number that comes next
in the scheme. The final part of the identifier referred to the subject of the document. Documents that superseded earlier ones
were indicated by numerals in parentheses following the sequence number. The editors frequently found documents that
superseded earlier ones but could not find the ones that had been
replaced. They concluded that undoubtedly some of these were
issued while others seemed to have been recalled before they
left the Secretariat.[14]

The Research Publications staff spent two years evaluating the
project before Freedman decided that the apparent difficulties
could be overcome and he made a commitment to microfilm the
League of Nations documents. A formal agreement between
Research Publications and the United Nations Library was
signed in 1969. In retrospect, Freedman says "had I known then
what I know now, I never would have done it."[15]

Faced with more than 25,000 documents and document sets,
the editors had to decide which were most appropriate for inclusion in the microfilm collection. They also had to devise a format
for the presentation. It was at this point that Research Publications recruited Harry M. Winton who had just retired from his
position as chief of the document reference section at the Dag
Hammerskjold Library at United Nations headquarters in New
York. Winton acted as initial editor of the project. It was he who
devised the format which Research Publications would use in
preparing the microfilm edition. The editors had decided that,

while the chronological and serial order in which the documents were arranged at the United Nations Library was "appropriate for an archival record," it would be a "great disadvantage to the historical researcher who ordinarily wants to go after materials on a subject rather than a strictly chronological basis."[16]

The formula Winton devised to overcome this problem was classification of the documents by subject matter. They then would be arranged chronologically within each category and organized by the source of the document: the Assembly, the Council, or a circular letter. Winton took on the task of bibliographically sorting the documents into subject categories.

From the start, it was not thought possible to include all of the documents in the collection. However, there was no question but that the 23,000 documents of the Assembly, the Council, and the circular letters would be filmed.[17] But the editors had to choose among the documents produced by the commissions and committees, the smaller document series emanating from the Secretariat, and the League's serial publications. In evaluating the documents prepared by the commissions and committees they finally decided "to select the documents of the one Commission of the League whose activities had perhaps the most historically interesting and continuing significance for the study of the sorts of international activities undertaken by the League."[18] Accordingly, the editors settled on the documents of the Permanent Mandates Commission which had supervised the division and administration of the various colonial spoils of World War I. They reasoned that a study of these documents along with the *Reports of the Mandatory Powers of the League* was indispensable in charting the history of "this officially sanctioned neocolonialism."[19]

It was also decided to include a rare set of the minutes of the directors meetings for the period 1919–1933 which had been unearthed accidentally at League archives in Geneva. The minutes and an attached group of confidential circulars originally existed in mimeographed and typescript form. They were regarded by the editors as especially valuable on the grounds that "they permit the historian to glance inside one of the most sensitive policymaking arenas of the League of Nations. They are a basic resource for writing the history of the League 'from the top down.' ''[20]

Of the League of Nations' serial publications, the editors selected the twelve they deemed most important. They justified their decision on the basis of the ''intrinsic worth of the materials themselves, both from the standpoint of the history of the League as well as twentieth century history in general.''[21] Another consideration was the need for archival copies of the serials since most were printed on poor quality paper that had already begun to deteriorate. The twelve publications selected were:

1. Annual Epidemiological Reports, 1922–1938

2. Armaments Year Book, 1924–1939/1940

3. International Health Year Book, 1924–1932

4. Memoranda on Production and Trade, 1926–1945

5. Money and Banking, 1913–1944

6. Official Journal of the League of Nations (including the Records of the Assembly and the Minutes of the Council), 1920–1946

7. Reports of the Mandatory Powers to the League

8. Review of World Trade, Balance of Payments and International Trade Statistics, 1910–1945

9. Statistical Year Book of the League of Nations, 1926–1942–1944

10. Statistical Year Book of the Trade in Arms, Ammunition and Implements of War, 1924–1938

11. Treaty Series, 1919–1947

12. World Economic Survey, 1931/1932–1942–1944

At the outset, the United Nations Library had agreed to allow Research Publications to remove the bindings from one of its three sets of League documents to facilitate filming. The first task was to go through the unbound set and list every missing document number. The editors then attempted to fill the gaps by checking the other two sets in the library for the missing documents. Gaps still remaining were then filled by searching the archives of the League of Nations in Geneva. The net effect, according to Reno, was "to constitute a union set of documents on microfilm which is more complete than any of the discrete sets and undoubtedly the most complete set of these League documents now in existence."[22] The actual filming did not begin until all the documents available in both New York and Geneva had been searched. In planning the project, Freedman had decided first to film the unbound documents at the United Nations Library and then the other documents available there to fill the gaps in the original working set. The last stage was to film the documents in Geneva.[23]

Because so much material had to be added to the first set of documents filmed, the actual production of the completed version required delicate handling. The master print had to be spliced many times to insert missing documents filmed after the gaps in the first set had been identified. In keeping with established Research Publications practice, the original was not used to produce the distribution copies. Instead, a second-generation (duplicate) silver halide film was made from the master, which has been preserved as a backup copy should anything happen to the working master.[24]

From the outset, the editors had planned to publish a hard copy guide to the microfilm collection. However, just what would be involved in this part of the project did not become obvious until the actual filming began. Errors in the League's numbering scheme, the complexities of its first short-lived numbering system, and the fact that many of the documents had never been assigned formal titles by the League required much more editorial work than had originally been anticipated.[25]

The numbering errors were the first to come to light. Some were simply printing mistakes and were easily remedied.

Others, however, required the editors to make some "highly complex judgments" in shifting a document from the subject category to which the League had assigned on the basis of the contents.[26] Where these errors occurred, the editors added to the League's identifying scheme a bracketed numeral indicating to which category, in their judgment, the document correctly belonged. In his introduction to the *Guide* Reno explains the "conservative rule of thumb" the editors followed in making these judgments:

> ... if there is *any* reason to think that a particular document *might* have been prepared by the particular section of the Secretariat whose printed category mark it bears (rather than by the section into which the document would fall more naturally, given its actual subject matter), the document has been left in the former category. In any case (the form used) preserves both the original form of the category number as well as the judgment of the editor that the document *really* belongs, because of its subject matter, in a different category.[27]

Other, more easily resolved errors involved omissions of the official number and insertions of a handwritten number taken from the French version of the document and the assignment by the League of the same number to two different but related documents.[28]

The errors which the editors found "potentially the most controversial" involved the omission of an "A" or "B" designation in those categories where both a letter and a numeral were used for identification—categories IA, IB, IIA, IIB, VIA, VIB and XIIA, and XIIB. Here, the most difficult problems concerned categories II(A) and II(B). In his introduction, Reno explains why:

> Part of the problem is inherent in the obvious relatedness of the subject matters of these two categories. Financial (IIA) and Economic (IIB) questions, however distinct they may be at their respective ends of the spectrum, tend to get inextricably intertangled with one another as they move towards the center. . . .

The other half of the problem . . . arises from the fact that the Financial Section and Economic Intelligence Service (IIA) and the Section of Economic Relations (IIB) were not always formally distinct sections of the League. So, technically speaking, there were, until their formal separation, no IIA and IIB documents at all; there were only II documents. The problem is compounded by the fact that even though a functional separation had taken place by 1923, the League itself did not begin to assign A and B designations with any frequency until 1931. Accordingly, some of the present *Guide's* assignments of A's and B's to category II documents are *retrospective,* and have as their primary justification a desire to maintain the subject classification of the documents as much as possible.[29]

Some documents completely lacked a category designation assigned by the League. In some cases, an error of omission was involved; in other cases, the League simply did not assign category markets to any of its documents prior to 1921.[30]

The chief difficulty involved in changing or regularizing a number—apart from the editorial judgment involved—was the fact that many of the decisions were made long after the document in question had been filmed. Since many of these documents were no longer available for refilming, the editors were unable to modify the number on the microfilm version of the document. In these instances, the editors had little choice but to modify the number for the purposes of compiling the *Guide* and hope that users, noting the presence of brackets in the *Guide* and their absence on the document itself, would realize that the two numbers referred to the same document.[31]

The fact that the League's first official numbering scheme differed substantially from the one adopted in 1921 and followed thereafter further complicated the editorial work on the *Guide.* The early schemes, the editors found, were "complex, sometimes redundant, and given to sudden and seemingly arbitrary changes."[32] Here, the editors had to devise an identification number compatible with the League's later scheme and cross-reference the original number to the editorially supplied identifier.

Resolving the problems presented by errors in the numbering schemes was only a prelude to an even more time-consuming phase in the preparation of the *Guide*. This concerned the description of each document and/or document set contained in the microfilm collection. Originally, the editors contemplated identifying each one by its number, by the place and date of issue, and by the formal title assigned it by the League. It was assumed that the title would serve as an adequate description of the subject matter. In his introduction, Reno explains why this was not to be:

> This bark of wishful thinking completely foundered on the shoals of the League's own vagaries and inconsistencies in titling, as well as on the rocks of lack of titles altogether—a frequent problem with archival materials. It was therefore necessary to actually search and, in many cases, read fully through the documents in order to determine what might function as a title.[33]

The editors, then, were required to devise a title for each entry in the collection. These "subject titles" were designed to cover not only the controlling document but also all other documents comprehended by a given entry.[34] Despite the care taken in the assignment of subject titles, the editors felt that a short title would not adequately describe many of the documents. Accordingly, they proposed preparing descriptive abstracts for each microfilm entry. This task had not been foreseen at the outset. Freedman sees it as the single most important factor causing the preparation of the collection to far exceed both the time and the money Research Publications Inc. originally had allocated to complete work on the project.[35]

The abstracts were designed to give researchers as concise an indication as possible of the substantive contents of each document or document set. However, the editors did not attempt to abstract each and every document in multi-document sets. Instead, where the number of documents in a set exceeded two or three or more, they were grouped together under a common description with beginning and ending dates, where available, for the time span covered.[36] Each abstract, however, was designed to summarize the subject matter, note the separate points covered where pertinent, and signal that the documents being described were "lengthy," "extensive," "very extensive," or "with statistical data."

The preparation of the microfilm collection of the League of Nations documents and its accompanying *Guide* far exceeded Research Publications' original timetable and budget. Four years elapsed from the project's official inception (1969) to the publication of the first volume of the three-volume *Guide* (1973). Volume 1 covers Assembly, Council, and circular letter documents in categories IA through IV. The second volume, completed in 1974, covers categories V–VII, plus the early classification numbers for the years 1919–1920 and the documents of the Permanent Mandates Commission. The third volume covers the remaining subject categories VII–XIII, plus G, General Questions (or those not falling into any of the other seventeen categories), as well as a master list of all document numbers included in the collection.

Since the project took so much longer to complete and so far exceeded its budget, Freedman was forced to adjust the original offering price and to concede that he had seriously undervalued it. When the full collection plus the *Guides* became available in 1975, the price was set at $8,900, which represented a substantial increase over the amount at which it had been initially advertised. The final product gives some indication of the scope of the project: 586 reels of microfilm, plus the weighty three-volume *Guide*.

Assembling the League of Nations documents on microfilm solved problems for researchers and librarians alike. Catharine Reynolds articulates the librarians' point of view in her review article:

At long last a publisher has come forward to collect, calendar and microfilm the League of Nations documents and serials, an essential source collection not found complete in any one library, and in all libraries seriously depleted by the ravages of time, bad paper, loss or inaccessibility through faulty organization of the collection.[37]

However, Reynolds cautioned libraries against discarding worn holdings of hard copy before checking them against the microform collection to insure that all of the documents had been reproduced:

> Collections bound with the World Peace Foundation title pages and content sheets contain sales publications, both with and without official numbers, and not all are included in the RPI project. Individual documents must be checked with the master index one by one.[38]

In her generally favorable review of the microform collection, Reynolds took issue with the arrangement of the *Guide,* noting that

> From the viewpoint of the librarian who must locate a single document, an archival arrangement by official distribution number would be preferred. For the scholar who must consult a number of documents in pursuit of his research, the new arrangement will enable him to follow his subject with a minimum of reel changing.[39]

Even more important from the point of view of the scholar is the accessibility to League of Nations documents made possible by the microfilm collection and its *Guide.* Before its existence, even those researchers who did travel to Geneva to study the League documents encountered difficulties due to the lack of a comprehensive index. As mentioned above, prior to the publication of the *Guide,* the only bibliographic tools available were Carroll's *Key,* Aufrict's *Guide to League of Nations Publications,* and the League's own two-volume *Catalogue.* However, since these resources limited themselves to documents placed on public sale by the League, they were no help at all when it came to the thousands of documents not formally published and sold.

With the micropublication of the League of Nations documents, historians, political scientists, students of international law, and others delving into the events and issues that occupied the world between World War I and II have had access to a wealth of material they would otherwise have to bypass. In his introduction to the sales brochure describing the Research Publications collection, Yale University History Professor Hans W. Gatzke speculates on the uses to which the microfilm collection can be put:

> The study of international relations between the two World Wars has been materially aided in the past by the official documentary collections prepared by all the major and some of the minor powers of the period. For financial and other reasons, the United Nations will never be able to complement these national series with a comparable collection of the League of Nations documents. It is in place of such an official collection that the League of Nations Documents and publications project fulfills a major function. Far too rarely have historians, when dealing with international problems of the interwar period, included the often significant dimension of League policy. With the easy availability of these important sources, such oversight henceforth can no longer be excused. Besides diplomatic historians, those interested in the domestic affairs of any of the League members will also find much of the interest in the material presented here. The definitive history of the League of Nations itself, as well as of some of its agencies and organizations, still remains to be written. But the League's experience is of interest not merely to historians. Political scientists, students of international law and international organizations, theoreticians as well as practitioners in such diverse fields as international finance, public health, economic integration, underdeveloped regions, and even that most recent concern—the environment—will find a wealth of information on their specific interests easily available in this solid primary resource. It provides a basis for fruitful research on a wide range of significant subjects.[40]

In offering its League package to libraries, Research Publications made it available in whole or in part and took the unusual step of offering the *Guide* independently of the microform collection. The rationale behind this decision was that the *Guide* itself was a valuable research tool. Indeed, in her review of the collection, Reynolds noted that although the *Guide* "is designed to be used with the microform collection, it could be used by a scholar without the film to identify the subject content of a document cited in another work or to scan publications of the League in a particular field of interest during a given time period."[41] However, Reynolds did express some misgivings about the *Guide*. She cited the lack of a subject and author index and the difficulty entailed in following the work of a committee except by establishing the beginning date and distribution number of its first report and then scanning every entry under the broad subject group, "a time-consuming and sometimes futile search since not every report was published as a separate document."[42] Another criticism she leveled related to the lack of cross-referencing from sales numbers or from symbols of other groups which, if encompassed by the project, are included only on the basis of their publication in the A, C, or CL classifications. To find out if a commission publication is included in the microform collection, she explained that

> it is necessary to consult either the official sales catalogs or the Carroll *Keys* to see if the publication was also assigned a number in the A, C, or CL series, which can then be located through the numerical index of the RPI *Guide*. When a document is not listed in either source, one can consult the numerical indexes to the *Official Journal,* but these did not begin publication until the mid 1920s.[43]

On balance, however, Reynolds recommended the collection for

> all libraries with research needs in political science, economics, and other areas of interest in the league period because it includes a large amount of material that cannot be found except by travel to the United Nations libraries in both New York and in Geneva and because the project is organized in a logical way, which makes individual groups

of publications easier to use. It is strongly recommended for research libraries which do not already have league collections, libraries with incomplete collections, and as a backup copy for a collection in poor physical condition.[44]

A notable exception to the League of Nations documents published by Research Publications is the collection pertaining to the work of the judiciary arm of the League, the Permanent Court of International Justice. The Court, with headquarters in the Hague in September 1921, was established by a protocol signed by the representatives of forty-two members of the League of Nations and ratified by twenty-nine of them. The court was created in response to the desire to settle international disputes on the basis of a body of law. It succeeded the Permanent Court of Arbitration which acted on disputes through a process of arbitration, not adjudication. In creating the court, the League specified in Article 14 of its convenant that it (the court) "shall be competent to hear and determine any dispute of an international character which the parties thereto submit to it. The Court may also give an advisory opinion upon any dispute or question referred to it by the counsel or by the Assembly."[45]

Over the years of its existence, the Court has handed down a series of judgments and advisory opinions on the cases brought before it. In planning the publication of the League of Nations documents, Research Publications deliberately omitted those papers stemming from the work of the court. Here, the reasoning was simple enough: the Court functioned separately from the other arms of the League, and its work was unrelated to the day-to-day business of the Assembly, Council, and Secretariat. However, following the micropublication of the League of Nations documents Research Publications in a separate project published in microfilm the publications of the Permanent Court of International Justice.[46]

The collection includes the judgments, orders, and advisory opinions rendered by the court as well as the pleadings and oral statements presented before it. Acts and documents relative to the organization of the court, as well as its annual reports,

1922–1945, complete the collection. Research Publications prepared a printed reel index to the publications in addition to filming four volumes of general indexes.

The micropublication of these Court documents enhances the accessibility of materials pertaining to the influence of the League of Nations and its judiciary branch during the period between the two world wars. For the legal scholar, the collection of the publications of the Permanent Court of International Justice provides increased opportunities for study of the first attempts to settle international disputes on the basis of law and to introduce the concept of advisory opinion in international jurisprudence. Between the two collections, scholars have a valuable resource for their research into the short but turbulent period between the two great wars.

NOTES

1. Robert C. Binkley, *Manual on Methods of Reproducing Research Materials: A Survey Made for the Joint Committee on Materials for Research of the Social Science Research Council and the American Council of Learned Societies* (Ann Arbor, Mich.: Edwards Brothers, 1936), p. 196.

2. Catharine J. Reynolds, "League of Nations Documents and Serial Publications, 1919–1946 Review Article," *Microform Review* 2 (1973): 272–73. It should be noted that Reynolds is cited heavily in this chapter for two reasons: she is an acknowledged expert in the field of government documents, and her review of this collection is the only one published to date.

3. Interview with Samuel Freedman, August 12, 1976.

4. Edward A. Reno, *League of Nations Documents, 1919–1946, A Descriptive Guide and Key to the Microfilm Collection* (New Haven, Conn.: Research Publications, Inc. 1973), p. x.

5. Ibid., p. xi.

6. Ibid., p. xii.

7. Hans W. Gatzke, "Introduction" to pamphlet entitled *League of Nations Documents and Serial Publications, 1919–1946* (New Haven, Conn.: Research Publications, Inc., not dated), p. 2.

8. Interview with Samuel Freedman, August 12, 1976.

9. Ibid.

10. Reynolds, "League of Nations Documents and Serial Publications," p. 272.

11. Interview with Samuel Freedman, August 12, 1976.

12. Ibid.

13. Reno, "League of Nations Documents," p. viii.

14. Ibid., p. xiii.

15. Interview with Samuel Freedman, August 12, 1976.

16. Reno, "League of Nations Documents," p. ix.

17. Ibid., p. x.

18. Ibid.

19. Ibid.

20. Ibid., p. xi.

21. Ibid., p. xii.

22. Ibid., p. ix.

23. Interview with Samuel Freedman, August 12, 1976.

24. Reynolds, "League of Nations Documents and Serial Publications," p. 274.

25. Reno, "League of Nations Documents," p. x.

26. Ibid., p. xiv.

27. Ibid.

28. Ibid., p. xv.

29. Ibid.

30. Ibid.

31. Ibid., p. xvi.

32. Ibid.

33. Ibid., p. xviii.

34. Ibid., p. xx.

35. Interview with Samuel Freedman, August 12, 1976.

36. Reno, "League of Nations Documents," p. xix.

37. Reynolds, "League of Nations Documents and Serial Publications," p. 272.

38. Ibid., p. 274.

39. Ibid.

40. Gatzke, "Introduction" to pamphlet, p. 2.

41. Reynolds, "League of Nations Documents and Serial Publications," p. 277.

42. Ibid., p. 276.

43. Ibid.

44. Ibid., p. 277.

45. Covenant of the League of Nations.

46. The collection consists of the publications series A through F, including Judgments; Advisory Opinions; Pleadings; Oral Statements and Documents; Acts and Documents Relative to the organization of the Court; Annual Reports; and General Indexes.

7

CONGRESSIONAL INFORMATION SERVICE'S INDEX TO CONGRESSIONAL DOCUMENTS AND MICROFICHE SERVICE

The need for indexes and finding aids to provide more than mere physical access to materials published in microform has been emphasized repeatedly throughout this examination of the history of scholarly micropublishing. The previous chapter discussed the difficulties inherent in assembling and indexing a large collection of historical documents. The case study presented in this chapter deals with a large body of contemporary research material: the transcripts, reports, and other documents published by the Congress of the United States in the course of its legislative duties. It illustrates how a major research gap was perceived and rectified, and describes how micropublishing can work in harmony with a computer-generated index to disseminate information.

The story of Congressional Information Service's Index to Congressional Documents and Microfiche Service is essentially one of entrepreneurial initiative in the tradition of Eugene Power, Albert Boni, and Samuel Freedman. It must begin, however, with a brief discussion of the information-gathering capability of the U.S. Congress.

In the course of its legislative duties, Congress studies the issues ranging from disarmament to drug abuse, from the protection of fish and wildlife to peanut allotments and proposals to build colonies in space. The introduction of legislation sets into motion procedures whereby Congress attempts to gather and evaluate all relevant information on the issue at hand so that it can decide whether or not the proposed law is necessary. This process brings into play the enormous resources Congress has at its command to explore virtually any issue of national and/or regional interest. Indeed, a by-product of Congress' information-gathering activities has been a huge body of research material invaluable to scholars, lawyers, businessman, and journalists. Until recently, however, the information assembled by Congress in the course of the legislative process—and at the expense of the taxpayers—has been largely inaccessible. None of it had ever been indexed, and for all practical purposes the public record of the public's business had been lost.[1]

A combination of circumstances were responsible: the relationship between Congress and the Government Printing Office (GPO), its printing arm; the budgetary limitations of individual congressional committees; the fact that neither the Library of Congress nor GPO has the authority or resources to index the transcripts of the hundreds of hearings held annually by the committees and subcommittees of the House and Senate; and a haphazard distribution system that prevents even the nation's depository libraries from assembling complete collections of congressional documents.[2]

This was the situation editor James B. Adler stumbled upon in 1968 when he innocently asked a librarian for the index to congressional hearings and learned there was none. The need was so obvious and the gap so astounding to him that Adler determined almost immediately to provide commercially what the government had failed to provide at public expense. In 1969, he founded Congressional Information Service to publish a monthly index to congressional documents and to distribute, on microfiche, a complete collection of hearing transcripts.

Any discussion of Adler's contribution to scholarly micropublishing must begin with a glance at how Congress gathers the information it uses to make its legislative decisions. At the heart of this process is the committee system—the conduit through which all proposed legislation must travel en route to passage.

After a bill is introduced in either the House of Representatives or the Senate, it is referred to the appropriate committee which, in turn, may refer it to a subcommittee. Before it can go to the floor of either house for debate, it must be approved by the committee which may recommend it as introduced, amend it, or rewrite it completely. If a committee chooses not to act on a bill, it may be stalled indefinitely.

Central to the committee's work are the hearings conducted to give members a chance to hear the views of all interested parties to a piece of legislation. Witnesses may include technical and academic experts, federal agency administrators, public and private interest groups or individuals, and elected state, local, and federal officials.

Committees may also call hearings purely for investigative purposes when no legislation is under consideration and may require (occasionally reluctant) witnesses to appear. The Watergate hearings in 1973 were conducted by a select committee established by the Senate to investigate the White House scandal triggered by the break-in at Democratic National Committee headquarters at the Watergate office building in Washington, D.C. No specific legislative proposals were before the committee when it opened its nationally televised hearings on May 17, 1973.

The number of congressional committees and subcommittees fluctuates from year to year. There are, however, seventeen standing committees of the Senate and twenty-one of the House. Operating under them are a host of subcommittees, some permanent and some established under specific directives for a limited period of time. In addition, there are special committees in each house and various congressional commissions and joint committees composed of members of both houses. Select committees are appointed by either house as the need arises; they exist for a period specified when they are created, and they operate under authority restricted to the matter they were organized to consider. All told, generally about 300 committees and subcommittees are active during each session of Congress. Hearings are their principal business: a Commission of the Operations of the Senate reported early in 1977 that Senate committees and subcommittees held more than 2,700 hearings in 1976.

Considerable manpower is assigned to the committees to carry out the preliminary work leading to hearings. Each committee and subcommittee has its own staff, and in addition, each member of Congress has a staff that may be drawn upon to assist in committee work. The committees and subcommittees utilize the facilities of the Library of Congress' Congressional Reference Service; they may request special studies by private organizations; they may seek out and consult expert witnesses and may require federal agencies to provide information.[3]

Most hearings are designed to gather opinions and information regarding the desirability of the legislation under consideration. However, as noted above, a committee will occasionally hold hearings even when no legislation has been introduced. These sessions are conducted in order to develop information needed for new or modified legislation in a given field, to fulfill annual oversight responsibilities concerning specific federal agencies or programs, or to investigate specific reports or charges of executive branch activities running counter to congressional intent or the public interest.

No matter what the purpose of the hearing, the end result is the collection of a great deal of information that might otherwise never have become public knowledge. Aside from the views and expertise of the witnesses, presentations may include the texts of reports related to the subject matter of the hearing, statistical analyses, correspondence, exhibits, and articles. Indeed, the record of a congressional hearing frequently brings together the most current and relevant information on matters of public concern.[4]

GPO publishes full transcripts of these hearings. They constitute the only official record of what transpires at the hearings as well as an authoritative source of research material for virtually all fields of interest. Unfortunately, however, the publication is frequently haphazard; indexing, until CIS was established in 1969, was nonexistent, and the distribution system by which the transcripts were to be made available to the public has never been dependable. Prior to 1970, access to hearing transcripts was at best "limited," for in addition to the lack of an index the table of contents was inadequate and, even worse, there was no

central source of information on what had and had not been published. Furthermore, nowhere were the transcripts fully cataloged.[5]

This situation is the outgrowth of the relationship between
Congress and GPO, a legislative agency that executes orders for
printing and binding placed by Congress and the departments of
the federal government. Hearing transcripts are published at the
request of the committee concerned. GPO does not have the
authority or the resources to prepare indexes, or even to catalog
the transcripts, without the permission of the committee that
issued the documents. For this reason, there is no central source
of information on what has been published. Even congressmen
and senators are not always kept informed when the committees
or subcommittees to which they belong issue new documents.
Nor, for that matter, are most committee staff members kept up
to date. Under these circumstances, it is small wonder that until
1970 much of the information gathered by Congress at enormous
public expense was as good as lost.

Distribution of the transcripts is also problematical. The documents are supposed to be made available to the public through
the U.S. government depository library system to which more
than 1,000 libraries belong. However, fewer than 100 of these
maintain complete collections of depository documents, and
even the so-called full depository libraries receive only about 75
percent of the congressional output.[6]

The full extent of this congressional information gap was not
immediately apparent to Adler in 1968 when, as a representative
of the R. R. Bowker Company, a reference book publisher, he
was seeking to develop nonfiction trade books with a Washington focus. Indeed, it was only by accident that he learned of the
lack of an index during the course of his own research at the
Hofstra University Library: "When I was told that there wasn't
one, I assumed at first that the Hofstra library just didn't have it
or that the librarian wasn't aware of it."[7]

On his next trip to Washington, Adler visited the Library of
Congress to check with the Legislative Reference Service (now
the Congressional Reference Service). "They told me that while
there definitely was a need for such an index they didn't have

either the staff, the budget or the authority to provide one," Adler recalls. He went home with the idea of publishing an index commercially but soon found that it was easier said than done: "It took me a year to figure out what form it should take. I was dealing with an incoherent body of literature. Nothing was standardized. The publications ranged from one page to thousands of pages."[8] Eventually, Adler came to the conclusion that the answer was not simply to index but to prepare what he describes as an "indicative abstract"—one that would tell the researcher what information was there but would not substitute for the document itself.

Operating out of the basement of his home in Roosevelt, New York, Adler worked up a pilot publication that he could show to librarians, his potential customers. He solicited criticism until he finally came up with a product that seemed to meet their needs:

> I then sent 5,000 to 6,000 copies to potential users asking for criticism. I got back an extraordinary response which was very useful when it came to polishing the product. On the basis of the response I was able to raise the money to put the operation on a businesslike basis.[9]

Adler moved to Washington in the summer of 1969 to establish the Congressional Information Service. He began to recruit a staff and to develop his sources of information on congressional publications. This entailed calling personally on the staff director of every congressional committee and subcommittee and enlisting their aid. Adler found that GPO (which he describes as "the most incompetent agency in the government") was of little help:

> The printing arm distributes material back to Congress; the publishing arm gets material from the bindery but doesn't know what it has. If you want 75 to 90 percent of what's being published, you can get it from the GPO, but if you want 100 percent, you don't have a chance.[10]

For example, GPO is not authorized to distribute committee prints, which Congress views as internal background information publications and which it does not distribute to the public. Committee prints may contain the reports on investigative and oversight hearings or may simply be printed as a record of information developed as a result of the ongoing research conducted by committee or subcommittee staffs into subjects of continuing interest to the committee or subcommittee.

Adler found that the only way to obtain 100 percent of congressional publications was via direct, personal, and regular contact with staff members. He offered a free subscription to his index as an inducement to cooperation and found that the response was excellent—limited only by the confidentiality of some documents or the knowledge of the staff about the publications issued.

Despite this cooperation, problems with document collections persisted. Adler learned, for example, that many congressional publications become "rare books" within weeks after they are printed and that rarely, if ever, are there reprints of out-of-print materials:

> A certain amount of Congressional literature becomes a rare book the moment it is issued. Some documents are printed in very small quantities and distributed only to members of Congress. There's a high percentage that is not distributed to people on the distribution lists. In addition, each committee decides on the quantity of documents published. But they operate under budgetary restraints which in some cases are a function of businesslike thinking and in others are a result of historical accident.[11]

This lack of availability of many congressional documents was one of the major considerations leading to Adler's decision to publish the congressional hearings in microfiche. Another was his discovery that fewer than fifty of the depository libraries received as much as 75 to 80 percent of congressional publications. He contends that there is no single library anywhere in the country that gets 100 percent. "I don't think we do," he adds, "but we do get substantially more than any other library."[12]

It was on the basis of this uneven distribution that Adler decided to publish the hearing transcripts on microfiche:

. . . if people wanted a complete collection of Congressional publications, they had to be made available in microform. It also was clear that it would be of no value to provide them in microform without access to their contents. When we started work on the index, we discovered almost immediately the need for a document delivery system to back up the index.[13]

The decision to publish the congressional hearings and other documents on microfiche was not without its own problems. Apart from the physical collection of the publications themselves and the difficulties of bibliographic control was the attitude of researchers and librarians toward microforms. In an interview, Adler described what the market was like when he launched his project:

In 1970 resistance to use of microforms in academic libraries was very high. We were dealing with a terribly unsophisticated market—librarians who were unaware of the difference between a positive and a negative format. However, by 1973 the pendulum had swung and library resistance to microforms was beginning to evaporate. In 1973 we exhibited at a political science conference in New Orleans. I spent the day in the booth dealing with faculty members—not with librarians. I expected them to look at the microfiche and say "Ugh. Microfiche. I can't stand it." But I got none of that. That's when I knew that the tough part was over. Users had come to conclude that they would rather have information on microfiche than no information at all.[14]

Apart from the initial resistance to the microfiche that CIS encountered among librarians, there was the problem of the actual production of the fiche transcripts. CIS did not at first produce the microfiche itself; it contracted the work to commercial suppliers. Adler found that this seemingly simple phase of the operation was fraught with difficulties. He explains CIS' needs:

We attempt to film to archival standards. We want decent
resolution and readable headers. All of this requires a great
deal of care. We have found, however, that not every
microform supplier is set up to meet the standards you'd
like them to meet. There's a great deal of difficulty in finding a supplier who would turn out a good quality product.[25]

Among CIS' special needs was quick development that combined both speed and quality control, but a supplier capable of
meeting that requirement was not easy to find. Initially, CIS
encountered what Adler now refers to as "a long catalog of
stupid things—mostly involving carelessness." In 1976, after a
trial-and-error period of switching from one supplier to another,
CIS decided to establish its own facility to produce microfiche.

A typical month's micropublishing produces between 350 and
700 master microfiche containing 25,000 to 50,000 pages of
material. An entire year's output is approximately 6,000 fiche
containing 450,000 pages. CIS makes its fiche available as a complete collection to replace or supplement a hard copy collection,
sells fiche "on demand" to customers who want copies of selected
hearings, or offers subscriptions to specially tailored collections
for customers who want just the publication of one or more specific committees.[16]

For all the difficulties initially encountered, the production of
the microfiche is relatively straightforward compared with the
preparation of the index. From an editorial point of view, the
project required stringent bibliographic controls, careful abstracting, and meticulous copy checks and proofreading. The im-
position of bibliographic controls was complicated by the fact
that each of the fifty-odd standing and joint congressional committees has authority to issue three to six different types of documents. These include:

1. *The transcripts of public hearings.* These may be published
in multiple volumes organized and numbered into two parts.
Occasionally, brief hearings concerning several unrelated pieces

of legislation may be pushed together in a single volume. The time lapse between the actual hearing and the issuance of the transcript may vary from a few days or weeks to as long as several years. Some committees assign serial numbers to their publications; others do not.

2. *House and Senate Reports.* These contain committee recommendations based on the findings of their hearings and deliberations. The reports accompany the bill to the floor. They may be brief, or they can include a lengthy and detailed analysis of each section of the legislation in question, as well as a careful explanation of the committee's reasoning on every significant point. They may include a separate summary of the issues involved or a history of the problem the legislation is designed to remedy. They may contain minority or supplemental views. Reports also emanate from conference committees established when the House and Senate pass different versions of the same bill and must reconcile those differences to the satisfaction of both houses. Reports may also be issued as a result of special investigatory or oversight hearings, field trips, or study panel investigations. They often include recommendations for new legislation or for revised federal agency procedures or policies. Reports are published quickly upon completion and are assigned sequential numbers within each house.

3. *Committee Prints.* As previously described, these are separate documents generated in the course of committee and subcommittee investigative and oversight activities as well as ongoing legislative research. These publications are not announced for public distribution and are viewed by Congress as internal working papers.

4. *Documents.* These include communications to Congress from the president and executive agencies as well as annual reports of some patriotic and veterans' groups, along with the texts of memorial tributes to certain individuals, and so on. In addition, some reports that may otherwise have been published as committee prints are published as documents.

5. *Executive Reports and Documents.* Such publications contain the text of presidential requests to the Senate to ratify a treaty or convention. They are lettered sequentially within each session of Congress and are issued swiftly upon completion.

6. *Special Publications.* These include publications that do not fall into any other category. They may be compilations of federal laws on a certain subject.

To keep track of these different types of documents along with the new information continuously being gathered by Congress, CIS devised a numbering system for use in both the index and the hearings fiche. In an article in the May 1971 issue of the *Journal of Micrographics,* Adler described the bibliographic controls CIS has instituted to keep track of the congressional publications it indexes and publishes in microfiche:

> . . . an accession numbering system in which the first four characters identify the committee and the type of document. For example, an accession number that begins "H501" identifies a hearing of the House Committee on Interstate or Foreign Commerce (or one of its subcommittees).

> . . . this system identifies and keeps together, in a single file, all the publications of the same committee and document type. In total, CIS maintains over 200 such open-ended files, in order to absorb and properly categorize all new documents as they are published.

> Our microfiche are identified according to the same accession numbering system as our abstracts; this enables each of our fiche subscribers to have a fully ordered and catalogued file of fiches at all times throughout the year.[17]

The assignment of the accession number is the first step toward publication once a document reaches the CIS offices. Next comes the preparation of the abstracts to be included in the index. Adler explains that CIS tries to say "in the fewest possible words enough to give the researcher a feel for what is in the document and to tell him precisely where he can find the significant charts, tables and related data."[18] Abstracts are written to sum up both the purpose of the hearing—the specific bill under consideration or the issue under study—and the subject matter covered in the course of each session. Individual abstracts sum up the testimony of each witness and include the affiliation of the witness. The index serves as a guide to both the microfiche and hard copy versions of the hearing transcript. It includes the GPO stock number, the classification number assigned by the superintendent of documents. There is also a page reference to indicate where an item of testimony can be found in the hard copy or fiche.

Most of the CIS editorial staff of between sixty-five and seventy persons is involved in the indexing and abstracting process. In building his staff, Adler initially sought editors with the experience to identify the salient details of testimony and with the patience to spend the working day studying one document after another. Now that CIS itself has had several years of experience, it trains its own editorial personnel.

Once the abstract is written, the editors must assign index terms to the testimony of each witness and to other elements of information contained in the transcript. Adler explains that the goal is to create enough references to every document so that no matter what the researcher's avenue of approach he will be led to the material he needs. He gives this example of how the index can be used:

Suppose, for instance he (the researcher) wishes to find all the congressional testimony of Ralph Nader published during 1970. Every witness before every congressional committee is indexed and each abstract indicates the pages on which the testimony begins and ends and where it can be found on the microfiche. During 1970, the *CIS/Index* published 15 abstracts of testimony given by Mr. Nader before 11 different committees and subcommittees. Each appearance is indexed, not only to the name, but also to the subjects that he discussed.[19]

In addition, CIS indexes to the authors and subjects of the significant articles, papers, and other exhibits that are inserted into hearing volumes; to the official numbers of the bills, law documents, and reports involved; to the official names of bills, laws, reports, and advisory bodies; and to the popular names of these publications and commissions, such as "Peterson Report" and "Rockefeller Committee on Department of Defense." The index also shows at a glance where every organization which testified before Congress stood on every issue and what each official of the organization said in his or her testimony.[20]

The actual publication of the CIS index is a computerized operation. Indeed, the product would not be possible were it not for computer software developed in 1970 that permits the processing of indexing information. The special computer software, according to Adler,

> enables us to input huge quantities of data in almost random order; to edit and correct with surprising speed and accuracy; to generate all our indexes without error; to maintain all our information in pure form independent of their typographic function codes; to call for a wide variety of type styles, limited only by the capabilities of the RCA Videocomp; and to operate on close deadlines.[21]

Once the editorial process is completed, the CIS editors enter the index information on a special data input form. It is then keyboarded onto magnetic tape which in turn is fed into the CIS-maintained data base in an IBM 360/40 computer.

The indexes themselves are generated via the manipulation of the data by the computer. This process checks every index term used in that particular issue against a separate file of thousands of potential cross-references so that only the appropriate cross-reference is used. Next comes the "composition run" during which the computer applies its typographic function codes to the index data. Finally, the data tape goes to an RCA Videocomp which produces fully made-up pages, vertically and horizontally justified, with folios, index-locators, running heads, and so on, in position.[22]

Although use of the computer makes possible the speedy publication of the CIS index, it does require a painstaking editorial process to detect and correct errors which the computer itself is incapable of identifying. For this reason, Adler explains, a typical index item receives nine editing and proofreading checks for style and accuracy before publication. All of this, including the initial assignment of accession numbers and the abstracting, takes place on a three-week computer deadline. CIS accepts the last documents for its monthly index on the last day of the month. Abstracting and keyboarding are completed during the following week, and the last stage in the process, the Videocomp, comes between the fifteenth and the twentieth of the month. The monthly issue is in the mail to subscribers between the twenty-fifth and the thirtieth.[23]

Although the preparation of the index is a streamlined operation, the hearings covered in each monthly issue usually took place three to four months before the CIS publication date. Thus, the index must await the release of the transcripts of hearings. There is no fixed timetable for when any hearing transcript goes to GPO for printing and binding or for when publication will take place. As noted earlier, there can be a time lag of as much as a year before the actual hearing and the publication of the transcript. In most cases, however, the delay is between three and four months.

The information gap that the *CIS/Index* and microfiche library fills is self-evident, given the failure of the government to catalog and index the hundreds of thousands of pages of information that Congress generates annually. As Adler states in his *Journal of Micrographics* article, "there is no single library in the country—including both the Library of Congress and the GPO's own library—which has a complete collection of documents for any given year."[24]

The CIS document collection system (there is a staff responsible for keeping track of congressional publications and acquiring documents as soon as they have been issued) has made possible the assemblage of a complete collection of congressional documents for libraries that want and need them. Even more important from a researcher's point of view is the access to congres-

sional information made possible by the index. Before publication
of the first monthly CIS index in 1970, a researcher looking for
information on, for example, drug abuse might be aware that a
congressional hearing on the subject had been held. To find out
when and by which committee, he would have to search the daily
schedule of committee hearings contained in the *Congressional
Record,* the transcript of action on the House and Senate floors.
The *Record* would tell him which committee had held the hearing and would list the witnesses, but that is virtually all the information given (other than the time, place, and legislation under
consideration). To learn what a specific witness had to say, the
researcher could consult newspaper accounts (if any had been
published) and could possibly find excerpts from testimony in
another publication, the *Congressional Quarterly* (a weekly magazine devoted to the activities of Congress). If the researcher were
in Washington, he might visit the committee's offices in an
attempt to get copies of statements presented by witnesses, but
only by consulting the official transcript would he get a verbatim
account of the testimony and the discussion between the witnesses and committee members.

But as has been noted above, access to a hard copy of the transcript may be impossible to come by: it may never reach the
depository library system. Even if it does, a researcher seeking
one item of information from a hearing transcript will have to
wade through possibly hundreds of pages before he locates the
testimony or discussion he wants to read. With the *CIS/Index,* all
he need do is look up "drug abuse" and check to see if the particular aspect of drug abuse in which he is interested is indexed. At
a glance, he can determine (1) the committee or subcommittee
that studied the issue; (2) the names of the witnesses who testified plus their affiliations; and (3) the topics of their individual
statements and discussion with committee members.

Finding the text of the testimony in which he is interested is
simplified by inclusion of the page numbers encompassed by the
statement and discussion of each particular witness. The microfiche headers supply the range of pages included on each individual fiche.

The variety of CIS clients gives an indication of the extent of interest in congressional publications: nearly 900 libraries, corporations, government agencies, trade associations, law offices, and research organizations subscribe. The cost of a subscription to the index varies according to the nature and budget of the library. For example, the most expensive subscriptions apply to corporate, trade association and law libraries, and libraries of foreign governments in the United States and Canada. The lowest subscription rate applies to libraries with an annual book and periodical budget of less than $30,000.

Given the fact that Congress routinely delves into matters pertaining to foreign aid, taxation, anti-trust, and other matters of vital interest to business, industry, special interest groups, and foreign governments, it is small wonder that the research arms of corporations, trade associations, foreign governments, and law firms maintain an ongoing interest in the activities of congressional committees. That these organizations welcome the access to congressional hearings provided by the *CIS/Index* and microfiche library has been well documented. In 1971, the *Law Library Journal* described it as "a librarian's and lawyer's dream . . . the year's most useful and most imaginative new library tool." After the appearance of the first index in 1970, the accolades poured in:

> . . . quite simply, a masterful major breakthrough in the congressional mazeway . . . offers to documents librarians, students, scholars and the laity, an access to information hitherto difficult or arduous to attain.[25]

> As more people get to know the *CIS/Index* . . . they will also become more familiar with the wealth of information that may be found in congressional publications and will find that the Documents Section of the Reference Department can provide them with hidden treasures.[26]

> . . . no effort in this area as ambitious, as enterprising, or as useful as the *CIS/Index* has been attempted. Researchers and librarians . . . will be astonished by this current biblio-

graphical *tour de force* . . . all scholars should be
interested.[27]

The reviewers and librarians were not the only ones impressed.
In 1971, after President Richard M. Nixon had appointed the
Commission on Federal Statistics, Adler was visited by a commission representative who wanted to know if CIS' experience
in indexing might be applicable to users of statistical data published by the federal government. The problem here, Adler explained, was that material was hard to find and that "much of it
was not even theoretically available. There was another common
denominator with our work with Congressional documents . . .
a lot of wheat and a lot of chaff and you never know which document someone will need tomorrow."[28] The end result of Adler's
discussions with the statistics commission was the publication
by CIS of the *American Statistics Index.* This product indexes and
describes nearly all government publications containing statistics—an output that exceeds 7,500 individual titles totaling more
than 900,000 pages of data. The statistics emanate from virtually
every federal agency as well as Congress.

CIS next took on another ambitious project: the microfilming
and indexing of the *U.S. Serial Set,* a major collection of congressional documents dating back to 1789. These include congressional reports and documents, along with some publications
from the executive branch and some from nongovernmental
agencies. Prior to the CIS effort, the serial set had never been indexed. Creating the index was a five-year project that required
the CIS staff to sift through 325,000 separate titles covering 11
million pages.[29] The index alone comprises twelve volumes.

The success of CIS in producing and marketing its indexes and
microfiche libraries speaks not only to the enterprise and skill
that Adler has exercised but also to the failure of the federal government to provide access to the publications upon which it
spends millions of dollars each year.

NOTES

1. Congressional Information Service, *The Working Papers of Congress* (Washington, D.C.: Congressional Information Service, 1975), p. 3.
2. Interview with James B. Adler, July 7, 1977.
3. Congressional Information Service, *User Guide* (Washington, D.C.: Congressional Information Service, 1975), p. 24.
4. *User Guide,* pp. 24–25.
5. Interview with James B. Adler, July 7, 1977.
6. James B. Adler, "Indexing as the Key to Micropublishing: The Case History of the Congressional Information Service," *The Journal of Micrographics* 4 (1971): 240.
7. Interview with James B. Adler, July 7, 1977.
8. Ibid.
9. Ibid.
10. Ibid.
11. Ibid.
12. Ibid.
13. Ibid.
14. Ibid.
15. Ibid.
16. Adler, "Indexing as the Key," p. 244.
17. Ibid., pp. 240–41.
18. Ibid., p. 242.
19. Interview with James B. Adler, July 7, 1977.
20. *User Guide,* p. xv.
21. Adler, "Indexing as the Key," p. 242.
22. Ibid., p. 244.
23. Ibid.
24. Ibid., p. 242.
25. Joe Morehead, "Review of CIS Index," *Reference Quarterly* (Winter 1970): 158–60.
26. Valerie R. Mullen, "Review of CIS Review," *Dartmouth College Library Bulletin* 13 (1972) (source, CIS brochure).
27. Unsigned review of CIS Index in *Choice,* 8 (1971): 200.
28. Interview with James B. Adler, July 7, 1977.
29. Ibid.

8

UNIVERSITY PRESSES
AND
MICROPUBLISHING

Micropublishing's pioneers dreamed that someday entire libraries could be contained on several reels of microfilm or microfiche. Over the years, such visions have given way to practical
realities, and the limitations of microforms as discussed in
earlier chapters, have become recognized. Both user resistance
and the inadequacies of viewing equipment have combined to
discourage most publishers from offering books and monographs
in microform instead of in hard copy. Only a handful of university presses have attempted to build upon the growing, if grudging, acceptance of the publication of research materials on
microform as an economic alternative to no publication at all.

This chapter presents three separate case studies examining
the efforts of three university presses—Chicago, the State of University of New York, and Toronto—to integrate micropublishing
into a book publishing program. Their experiments were initiated
despite the fact that the negative attitude of the academic community had already been documented. A 1959 report presented
to the American Council of Learned Societies concluded that
scholars and administrators were "insufficiently ready" to accept
micropublications on their merits, principally because of the
inconvenience entailed in reading them—the attendant eyestrain,
the need for a special reading device, and, perhaps most importantly, the fact that microforms defy "easy handling and contemplative reading or re-reading . . . (and preclude) useful marginal
notes and memoranda."[1]

Although these prejudices have not yet been overcome, in the years since that report was presented, microforms have achieved wide acceptance in the library and the academic world. Technological improvements have made reading easier, and the proliferation of micropublications and an appreciation of the economics of scholarly publishing have helped dissipate some of the early resistance. From a publishing point of view, this willingness to accept microforms came none too soon. Faced with spiraling costs that were forcing them to curtail their output, some university presses began to look toward original publishing in microform as an economically viable means of offering highly specialized works with a small sales potential.

The financial problems of the university presses and the academic libraries that constitute their market were summarized in 1974 by Norman Mangouni, director of the State University of New York Press (SUNY):

> Both are caught in a cycle of higher prices and reduced buying power that is progressively diminishing their capacities to function effectively. The result has been a communications paradox; deceleration of scholarly publishing activity at a time when the knowledge industry requires acceleration, especially in the flow of scientific and technical information.[2]

SUNY was one of the pioneers in the scholarly publication of original material in microform. In 1972, it brought out *The Gothic World*[3] by Brian T. Regan, the first book-length monograph produced exclusively in microfiche to be cataloged in publication[4] by the Library of Congress. At the time, several other university presses were beginning to experiment, among them the University of Chicago Press, the University Press of Kansas, Southern Illinois University Press, the University of Washington Press, and the University of Toronto Press.

The decision to publish in microfiche, Mangouni explained, represented an effort

> not merely to survive amid declining market conditions but to meet the challenges posed by the need for more and

faster publishing services. The advantages of speed and economy of production make it possible to bring out specialized monographs quickly, in a space-saving, low-postage format and at prices libraries can afford. A micropublication of the author's final typescript can be produced and placed into the stream of literature several months earlier than can a printed book, a fact of considerable importance to scholars.[5]

Indeed, as Mangouni noted, publishing economics were forcing university presses to cut back production and to turn down or even refuse to consider scholarly works that might have limited market potential because of specialized content, extreme length, color illustrations, or complex typographic features. This, in turn, made it difficult for many young scholars to become established in their disciplines and to advance their careers through the traditional medium of publication.

As a result, pressure to accept publication in microform began to emerge from various segments of the academic world. In an article in *PMLA*, the journal of the Modern Language Association of America, Pennsylvania State University professors Caroline D. Eckhardt and John B. Smith urged their colleagues to regard

as more respectable that we have forms of publication other than the traditional manufactured book or monograph. Publication by means of microfilm, microfiche, etc. may be the only means by which works with limited audience appeal can be produced under current market conditions. The number of reprint series via microfilm is increasing and might well be paralleled by microfilm series of original works.[6]

Another prestigious group, the Ad Hoc Committee on What to Publish, advised the Yale University Press to explore new ways of producing and distributing manuscripts that were narrow in scope or sales potential. Although the committee conceded that some of the alternatives to conventional monograph publishing appeared "uninviting and unimpressive to authors as well as to their critics and peers," financial considerations required that they be considered. The committee concluded that among the alternative formats available, microfiche "seems the most promising." It further suggested that if Yale took the lead in departing from conventional publishing formats, attitudes toward them "may eventually change so that scholarly books produced at lower cost will be judged by their content and not by their format."[7]

From a publishing point of view, the decision to present original research monographs on microfiche was based on considerations beyond the economic pressures. The University of Toronto's decision to experiment with simultaneous publication of fiche and regular format was based on three premises outlined in a 1975 article in *Scholarly Publishing* by press editor Ian Montagnes:

> One was that microfiche had at least become established in North America as a reference medium. A second was that microfiche is the logical medium for micropublication of books. These two still appear valid. The third was that information would continue to grow at a considerably faster rate than capital budgets for libraries, and that as the premium on shelf space grew, so too would the attractiveness of microform. We were correct in the first part of that belief.

> At the time, we argued that scholarly works are essential to a research library but spend much of their lives occupying expensive shelf space. Microfiche editions would save footage. (The Library of Congress had estimated it costs 50 percent less to store film than to store a book.) They would also make it possible for libraries to buy two copies, one (in book form) for circulation and the second (in microfiche) as a protection stack copy held at minimum storage costs.[8]

Despite these advantages and the academic community's apparent willingness to accept micropublication of original works, the optimism with which the experiments were launched does not appear to be justified by experiences to date. By 1977, Mangouni had lost some of his own enthusiasm, conceding that far from accepting micropublication as an alternative format "there is considerable resistance in the academic community toward even doing away with some of the conventions of book publishing." He went on to explain that

> the market is not willing to accept that microform is economically necessary even where sales potential is small. We even see resistance toward eliminating dust jackets on the conventional book even though it adds $500 to $1,000 to production costs—a significant percentage of the total cost. The authors resist the elimination and the marketplace does, too.[9]

Similar views were expressed by Morris Phillipson, director of the University of Chicago Press, and by Montagnes at Toronto who reported that "after an initial flurry" following Toronto's decision to issue new titles in microform at the same time as in regular book form "the number of orders for microfiche dwindled." Based on this experience and the lack of response to similar programs undertaken by other university presses, Montagnes concluded that "widespread use of fiches for scholarly publication, particularly outside the sciences, seems unlikely to occur for some few years."[10]

Based on Chicago's experiences, Phillipson was even more pessimistic in his evaluation of fiche as a format for the publication of monographs. In 1972, Chicago brought out on microfiche *Ranade and the Roots of Indian Nationalism*[11] by Richard F. Tucker. It received few reviews, and sales were disappointing— just over 100 copies were sold.

Resistance to the use of fiche for text publication at Chicago stiffened after a 1976 offer to provide in fiche or in Xerox form copies of the full text of articles printed only as precis in the *Journal of Modern History*. Of the twelve journal articles offered in the alternative formats, there were orders for only three in fiche compared to more than twenty orders for the hard copy Xerox reproductions of the typescripts. All told, Phillipson regards attempts to provide original textual material in fiche as a "complete flop," although he does concede that there was less resistance to the fiche format in the social sciences and physical and biological sciences than in the humanities.[12] Nevertheless, Chicago now regards the use of fiche for textual material as unsuitable and has abandoned plans to use it for any text publication at all, at least in the foreseeable future.

The failure of the market to respond to the publication of original materials in microform can be traced to several factors, among them the reluctance of researchers to work with materials available only in this medium; the lack of convenient equipment for the reading of microforms away from the library setting; the suspicion among scholars that materials published only in microform are not well enough regarded to be published in book form; and the fact that, from a buyer's point of view, the materials made available in microform are not necessarily less expensive than they would be in book form.[13]

The reluctance of researchers to use microform has been well documented over the years. One survey conducted in 1969 by Harold Wooster, elicited comments such as "everything about microfiche is marvelous—except reading it." Another user offered the opinion that microfiche is an "information burial system."[14] Still another study uncovered a universal dislike of working with microforms among people assigned to catalog them and provide bibliographic controls.[15] One authority in the field surveyed sixty libraries throughout the United States in 1974 and came to the conclusion that user resistance was understandable in view of the unsatisfactory conditions that persist in many libraries. The study found that most microform reading rooms were located in unattractive quarters in inconvenient areas of the library with inadequate light and cramped writing space, and were supplied with machines that were not kept in working order.[16] A 1976 survey by Knowledge Industry Publications confirmed that many libraries do not extend themselves where microforms are concerned: instructions on the use of machines may be unavailable or incomprehensively technical, and staff members often lack the time and patience to instruct patrons in the use of microform reading equipment and frequently neglect to tell patrons that microforms are available.[17] As Montagnes sums up the situation:

User resistance is . . . not perhaps unexpected by anyone
who has experienced the nausea and eyestrain of searching
for a reference on one of the older models of microfilm
reader. Common objections are: microform is unfamiliar
and hard to read; research must be done in the library
where the readers are kept; it's impossible to underline or
annotate the page; there's no way to have several pages
open at once for repeated reference; the user is physically
dependent on the reader and its bulb—which, as one reader
discovered, can blow out at 1 a.m. with no spare on hand.[18]

Some of the early resistance to microforms has been overcome
by the introduction of the portable microfiche reader that frees
the user from the library. Nonetheless, as Montagnes concludes:

Before microfiche are fully accepted, the industry is going
to have to produce reading equipment that is engineered
for convenient use, not only in the library but also at home
or in the office. Wooster coined the name "cuddly" to
describe the ideal portable home or desk viewer; and while
no one is likely to take a fiche to bed or into the bath, his
term sums up the concept of personal, informal use that
must be achieved before most of us can become comfort-
able with the new medium.[19]

In general, it appears that the greatest resistance to the use of
microforms is concentrated among older readers. Senior faculty
members, for example, are much more reluctant to accept the
medium than younger researchers. Several studies have confirmed that reader resistance appears to be related to age. Indeed,
in one study a test group of MIT students was offered free printed
or microfiche materials and given the opportunity to borrow
microfiche readers. After two years of growing familiarity with
fiche, they voted four to one in its favor as more convenient than
printed matter.[20]

While librarians in general reported fewer problems with
microfiche reading equipment than with microfilm readers,
Knowledge Industry Publications found that almost half of the
academic libraries responding to a survey conducted in connec-

tion with its study did not lend portable microfiche readers, even though 60 percent of the respondents said they did circulate microforms.[21] Since the price of portable microfiche readers is substantial—about $100—publishers are faced with what the *Chronicle of Higher Education* calls a "chicken or egg" dilemma:

> Users may be reluctant to invest in the reading machines until there are a lot of fiche to look at; publishers will be reluctant to put out many books . . . until there are a lot of buyers equipped to look at them.

> The price of the reading machines probably could be substantially reduced by mass production, but manufacturers may want to wait for a mass market. At the same time, there is not likely to be a mass market for the reading machines until they become less expensive.[22]

One reason Montagnes suggested for the lack of response to the University of Toronto Press' experiment with simultaneous publication of fiche was the squeeze on library budgets that coincided with the first attempts to make original materials available on microfiche. He explained that, in formulating the experiment, the press discussed its plans with a sampling of librarians interested in microforms and that they encouraged the experiment. He added, however, that "What we had not counted on was the tightening of library budgets which occurred almost simultaneously with the program and arrested its progress as well as that of scholarly publishing in general."[23]

Related to the budget squeeze were the pricing policies adopted by university presses in releasing their first micropublications. Toronto opted for selling the fiche at the same list price as the hard copy edition. Montagnes explained why:

> We took this stance on philosophical grounds defining the microfiche edition as extra run on copies of the printed book (which was used as camera copy). To price the fiche copies differently would have been no more logical than pricing the two-thousandth copy of the print version at less than the first copy. We feared it might also be unfair to the

author, who would receive less reward in royalties. Eventually, as a marketing experiment, we made a package offer which was in effect a 40 percent discount on the microfiche edition to anyone who bought both hard copy and fiche editions at the same time. The response remained minimal.[24]

In pricing its monographs published in microfiche, SUNY attempted to recover as much as possible of the development costs. *The Gothic Word* sold for $12.50. Total sales came to 120 copies, leading Mangouni to suspect that the monograph would have done much better and possibly would have recovered production costs had it been printed in hard copy. At Chicago, the strategy was to deliberately underprice the micropublications at $1 per fiche.

The failure of these early micropublications to recover their production costs discouraged all three of the university presses, which were the most active pioneers, from continuing to publish original materials exclusively in microfiche. The only exception to this policy is at the University of Chicago where a text fiche experiment (text in hard copy; illustrations on fiche) is still underway. (This project is described in detail following this discussion of scholarly publishing in microfiche.) Mangouni, Phillipson, and Montagnes all stress that, while it is theoretically possible to publish book-length monographs on microfiche when economics forbid publication in hard copy, costs preclude further experiments as long as the market remains small. Editorial costs are constant whether a manuscript is published in microform or hard copy: there is no change in the expense of editorial appraisal, both in house and by outside readers; there are the same costs for sales and promotion and of order fulfillment and counting. Mangouni explained in an interview that production costs normally come to about half the total cost of publishing a book in hard copy. It is on the other half—the manufacturing costs—that a publisher can save if he chooses microform as an alternative. Here, costs can amount to as little as 1 percent of the normal manufacturing costs for the first distribution copy of a monograph on microfiche from a 350-page typescript range from $25 to $30, roughly 1/100th the cost of composition, printing paper, and binding required for production of a hard copy. This savings could be a boon to a publisher: a press could avoid tying up scarce working capital in printed books which might not turn over quickly enough to yield an acceptable cash flow. The press could conserve funds for the publication of works of broader interest and great sales potential. And, since microforms can be produced on demand from film masters, the publisher can avoid the need for an investment in inventory. Furthermore, the publication could always be considered "in print" since microforms can be produced "on demand" from film masters. However, such publication remains uneconomic if sales are not high enough to recoup the money expended for the other production costs. But, as Montagnes reported,

> The market at present is also much, much smaller than for a book. As a result, the total unit cost in fiche is still extraordinarily high, unless there is a direct or hidden subsidy. One may argue, however, that the editorial costs would have to be subsidized regardless of the mode of production; that with fiche virtually no capital is tied up in inventory; and that the list price can be established to meet somewhat more than the normal provision for fixed overhead to help compensate for the short run.[25]

The editorial costs are inevitable inasmuch as university presses insist that all material be treated the same way, no matter what format is used. To reassure both authors and librarians that publication in microfiche as an alternative to hard copy does not mean that the work itself was considered unsuitable for book form, the University of Chicago Press set forth this policy in a 1972 promotional brochure:

> Every new work taken under consideration by this Press is treated to identical scholarly scrutiny both by the Press' editors and by scholar-referees in the field, whether it is eventually published in microfiche or in conventional form. The University of Chicago Press does not now, nor will it in the future, offer any work in microfiche that it would not, given the necessary financial resources, offer as a case-bound book.[26]

The attitude at SUNY was similar. Although it had not published an original work in microform for more than two years (as of the spring of 1978), SUNY followed a policy of informing the author that his or her work might be published in either fiche or paper. The decision as to medium was made after editorial and market appraisal and in accordance with prevailing budget considerations, but at the time, any work that passed the editorial board could be published. SUNY reported that, as its policy became better known, scholars began to submit specialized manuscripts specifically for microfiche. However, as a result of the disappointing response to its first micropublication, SUNY has more recently been issuing hard copy editions of as few as 300 copies using typescript prepared by the author as camera-ready copy.

Although Mangouni continues to believe that, ultimately, microfiche will become the only economically viable alternative for university presses as publication costs continue to soar, he does not think that microfiche will become a realistic medium of choice "until the point is reached that the market for printed books drops off so sharply that it is no longer feasible to bring out a printed book."[27]

Before that can happen, he said in an interview, the cost of producing a printed book will have to increase "like the price of coffee." In the meantime, he believes that many university presses will continue to curtail their output and to concentrate their resources on works with wide appeal that can be produced in sufficient volume to recoup their preparation costs.

Montagnes' views are similar:

As the economic crunch gets tighter—as it becomes less and less possible to publish books that are over 300 pages or will not sell, 500 or 2,500 or 3,000 copies—microfiche may look more and more attractive to publisher, author and reader. . . . Scholarly publishers have waded partway into the pond. The water is just off the chill and the depths are uncertain. But the prospect does have attractions, and the sun is too hot to stay out on the beach.[28]

While by 1977 plans for original publishing in microfiche had been postponed or abandoned, a few experiments continued. In April 1977, SUNY published on computer output microform a printout of research material for the study of Ruiziana (a word referring to Juan Ruiz' work "Libro de Buon Amourti"). But this kind of project also presented the publisher with problems inherent in dealing with one of the university's computer centers, in getting what Mangouni described as "high priced computer help committed to the project and in establishing priority for the programming and computer run time." "Whenever we ran into bugs," he reported, "we had trouble getting the programmers freed from higher priority projects. It took us several years to get the tapes through the hardware and software."[29]

At the University of Chicago, all micropublishing of original work in textual form has ceased. However, the press is continuing to experiment with a format it stumbled upon during its earliest attempts at micropublishing. It now offers a series combining text in hard copy with illustrations on microfiche. This text/fiche project was launched in 1972 with the publication of *Victorian Bookbindings: A Pictorial Survey* that includes fifty-two pages of text accompanied by three color fiche packaged in a hard cover.[30]

Phillipson explained that the press decided to experiment with the text/fiche format after it had been approached about a book on Victorian bookbindings in conjunction with an exhibit at the University of Chicago Library:

> The woman who put the exhibit together and had done the text for the catalog wanted to do a book based on it. Now there were 251 images of bookbindings that she wanted to reproduce—in full color! It was out of the question. A book like that would have to sell for at least $100. It was utterly preposterous. But by then we were using color fiche to supplement some of the books we were publishing—we provide the fiche in the back of some medical texts to illustrate tissue segments reproduced in black and white in the body of the text.[31]

The response to this first text/fiche offering was encouraging. The press sold more than 350 copies of *Victorian Bookbindings,* enough to generate interest in planning an acquisition program in the general areas of art history, archaeology, and anthropology. In its promotional material announcing the text/fiche program, the press reiterated its conviction that books are the only appropriate conveyors of the printed word and explained that the economics of publishing preclude the effective presentation of visual material in book form:

> The book . . . remains the most advantageous means of disseminating *written* documents. . . . The reader is free to interact with the printed page by writing gloss notes or underlining, and he can quickly find any sentence or paragraph by memory, bookmark, table of contents or index. . . .

> (But) to present visual materials effectively a book designer must often select a large page format to preserve pictorial detail. For the sake of the illustrations alone, *the entire printed form,* including pages carrying only words, must be expanded to a larger, more costly size. Both paper quality and binding costs will spiral, ultimately showing up in the list price of the book.

> To contain both price and bulk, publishers commonly restrict both the number and size of the illustrations. Ideas for books that would provide extensive visual documentation are shunned by publisher and author alike, or such books are produced in compromise fashion with only selective illustration.

> Books that are "profusely illustrated" in full color are even more costly to produce; they fall generally into two categories:

>> —very expensive books that few individuals can afford.

>> —books on subjects of such broad appeal that the many copies printed can share the heavy expense of full color printing.[32]

Text/fiche was introduced as an economic means of overcoming the limitations of presenting visual material in book form:

> When the advantages of the book are combined with the advantages of film—the natural medium for illustration— the limitations of the printed illustrated publication disappear. The text and captions are printed economically on an appropriate page size and the illustrations are carried compactly and inexpensively on film for enlargement by a microfiche reader.[33]

The first text/fiche projects were developed in conjunction with museums with collections that needed exposure to interested audiences. To develop the text/fiche publications, the press contracted with museums for both the preparation of the text manuscript and the photographs to be used on the fiche. It also worked with the Eastman Kodak Company to modify the standard 4 × 6 inch fiche to carry eighty-four instead of the standard ninety-eight frames. This adjustment was necessary to permit the fiche to carry both vertical and rectangular images. The fiche form arrived at has square rather than rectangular frames, so that the vertical and rectangular images can be intermixed at the same reduction ratio. The project also necessitated a search for an appropriate fiche viewer that could accommodate the square image format. Two were found suitable: a hand-held reader that retails for $34.95 and can be used to view the images with one eye, and a console reader with projection capacity that sells for $198.50.

Another problem concerned the life span of the color film used for the fiche which generally is shorter than that of a printed book. If handled improperly, fiche can pick up surface scratches. In addition, the electrostatic charges on the surface of the film tend to attract dust. Eventually, color fiche, like any color film, fades and loses its color fidelity. To determine whether the fiche could stand up well enough to justify an investment in the text/ fiche program, the press worked with film suppliers to test for durability and resistance to damage. Not all of the problems could be overcome, and users are advised to store the fiche under dark, dry, cool conditions to maximize the life span. Replacements for damaged and/or faded fiche are available from the press at $2 for black and white fiche and $5 for color.

The nature of the project demanded that the authors take special care in preparing the material for publication. The press provides an "author's guide" that gives detailed instructions for both the preparation of the text and the fiche. It stipulates that only original color transparencies will be accepted for publication and reminds authors that the quality of photographic materials submitted "ultimately will determine how true the fiche images are to the original art or object."[34] Accordingly, authors are instructed to omit photographic materials "that offer poor color fidelity, or those with insufficient color density. Also omit, whenever possible, high contrast photographs (details shown in shadow or highlight areas), images that are out of focus, those that are seriously under or over-exposed and those that have scratches, folds or stains."[35]

Authors are supplied with layout worksheets on which the sequence of images is to be indicated. Since images are not identified on the fiche itself, the authors must take special care to indicate clearly the proper order of the photographs submitted. Authors are responsible for indicating on the slide mount which is the top and which is the front of the slide, a necessary precaution to avoid having images printed upside down or backwards on the fiche. They are also requested to take the photographs at one time on the same kind of film and to process it in one batch. Black and white illustrations must be submitted in 8 × 10 inch low-contrast, matte finish prints that are not curled, folded, or scratched.[36] The explicit instructions for the preparation of the materials extend to the precautions to be taken in the mailing.

Insistence on the use of only original transparencies stems from the desire to provide the greatest color fidelity possible. Each successive film generation from the original increases color deviation and builds unacceptable contrast. Indeed, the color fidelity made possible by the transfer of original transparencies to fiche is one of the major selling points. Because of the inherent limitations of materials used in inks and paper, printed images can never reproduce the tonal ranges and exact colors captured by the dyes used in color film. Publishing in fiche details the full-color range and fidelity.[37]

In introducing the text/fiche project, Howard M. Levin, then assistant director of the press, explained that the format

> was the result of more than three years of experiments. We learned that microfiche should carry visual images only save for a "pagination" system and header information to identify the fiche. . . .
>
> Text/Fiche thus respects film as the natural carrier for pictorial material and the printed book as the most appropriate vehicle for words. The net result is a new form of illustrated book which greatly expands our capability for illustration reproduction and dissemination over that of more conventional film formats or the highly illustrated printed book.[38]

In addition to *Victorian Bookbindings*, the first collection of text/fiche publications included the following titles: *Cornhusk Bags of the Plateau Indians*, a selection of 1970 bags from the Cheney Cowles Memorial Museum of the Eastern Washington State Historical Society; *Pre-Columbian Art*, eighty-three color photos from the Dumbarton Oaks Collections; *British Masters of the Albumen Print* by Robert Sobieszek; *American Art in the Barbizon Mood*, 125 photographs from the National Collection of Fine Arts; *The 1905–1907 Breasted Expeditions to Egypt and the Sudan*, a two-volume publication containing more than 900 photographs; *Persepolis and Ancient Iran*, a collection of 1,000 photographs from the Oriental Institute; *A Collection in the Making*, 419 color reproductions of works from the Phillips Collection; and *Pottery Techniques of Native North America* by John Kenneth White.

The advantage of the text/fiche program to researchers in the arts is clear: it makes available for study color reproductions of paintings and artifacts that could never be included in a book for purely economic reasons.

Levin outlined the scholarly applications of the program in an interview with *Publishers Weekly:*

Esoteric fields such as archeology and botany have severe
illustrative problems—they have developed special nomen-
clature to describe through number and letter symbols
those things which might best be described visually and in
color, simply because the cost of printed color is so prohibitive.[39]

The project is also of special interest to art students, opening
up for them collections that may rarely be seen by the public. As
Levin explained:

Many museums typically show only about 15 percent of
their holdings in public displays at any one time. And
mounting a new display is a costly undertaking, so it is
done only at carefully chosen intervals. As a result, much
of the material held by museums actually never gets before
the public, and that which does is seen by only a small portion of the total potentially interested audience.

Text/Fiche publications can greatly extend the reach of a
museum. Collections which cannot be shown for lack of
display space can be photographed and organized into publications that can be disseminated worldwide. Similarly,
exhibits which cost a great deal of time and money can be
made, through such publication to live well beyond the
time they are actually shown in the museum. And finally,
collections can be shown in many ways to more than one
audience through the medium of Text/Fiche publication because the photographs of a given collection can be rear-
ranged in many sub-groupings and sequences to make different points, to relate to different interest groups and to
serve different purposes. Once the basic photographs are
available, different publications can be created by changing the pictorial sequences and writing new text.[40]

The initial response to the new project was enthusiastic. In a
review of *A Collection in the Making* in the *Art Library Society
North American Newsletter,* Caroline Kent reported that the photographic images "are more direct than printed color plates in a

book could be. On microfiche readers with two lenses, details may be enlarged. Whole paintings may be enlarged with little loss of color density." She concluded with a prediction:

> Scholarly color microfiche is here to stay. Many collections heretofore obscure will now be made available. Text/Fiche has published "the first Text/Fiche" publications list and all the offerings are tempting. The Phillips Collection is an excellent example of a high quality set at reasonable cost; printed reproductions of 419 color paintings would cost more than twice as much.[41]

The *Chronicle of Higher Education,* in an article reporting on the introduction of text/fiche, hailed its potential impact on higher education "both in teaching and in research," adding that "It could open to students a greater number of graphic materials, in wider variety and more accurate reproduction, than ever before . . . (and) it will offer researchers a chance to include full-color illustrations in conventional printed books."[42] The *Saturday Review* predicted an even greater impact in an "Artsletter" announcing the introduction of text/fiche: "(it) may do for the visual arts what the long-playing record has done for music."[43]

The major obstacle the program faces is what Levin at the time of its introduction called "the tempo of acceptance." If response is not favorable during the trial period, the project might have to be scuttled.[44] As Phillipson put it, the program depends on whether or not the art world resists microfiche as the academic community has: "We've introduced a whole new technology to a whole new audience. Most art people don't know what fiche is and they are having to learn."[45]

By the spring of 1977, response had been favorable enough to justify plans to add nine titles to the eleven already published. But the future of the program clearly hinged on the willingness of the "new audience" to accept text/fiche as a fitting substitute for the books no one can afford to print. Clearly, this compromise between publishing in microform or not publishing at all may prove a partial solution to the economic crunch faced by the university presses. It appears, however, that micropublishing has not yet proven to be an acceptable alternative to publication in book form no matter how esoteric the subject matter. Whether the harsh verdict rendered by the market in the three cases described here will someday be reversed by worsening publishing economics remains an open question for the future.

NOTES

1. Rush Welter, "The Publication of Books with Small Potential Sale, and Related Problems," in *Problems of Scholarly Publication of the American Council of Learned Societies* (New York: American Council of Learned Societies, 1959), p. 33.

2. Norman Mangouni, "Micropublishing Among the University Presses," *Microform Review* 3 (1974): 251.

3. This title was calculated as having limited sales potential of about 400 copies. Micropublication offered the only economical means of publication.

4. Cataloging in Publication (CIP) is a program whereby the Library of Congress provides participating publishers with the actual catalog card information for the respective title prior to publication.

5. Mangouni, "Micropublishing," p. 251.

6. Caroline D. Eckhardt and John B. Smith, "Facts of Scholarly Micropublishing: Book-Length Works on Literature," *Publications of the Modern Language Association* 89 (1974): 366.

7. Chester Kerr, "What to Publish at Yale," *Scholarly Publishing* 5 (1974): 216.

8. Ian Montagnes, "Microfiche and the Scholarly Publisher," *Scholarly Publishing* 6 (1975): 78.

9. Interview with Norman Mangouni, May 10, 1977.

10. Montagnes, "Microfiche," p. 79.

11. It is interesting to note that the University of Chicago Press neglected to send a review copy to *Microform Review*, the only journal that reviews scholarly micropublications for libraries.

12. Interview with Morris Phillipson, May 5, 1977.

13. This is a misconception that has hindered the development of original micropublishing. Just because material appears in microform does not mean it should be less expensive.

14. Harold Wooster, *Microfiche 1969—A User Survey* (Washington, D.C.: U.S. Air Force Office of Scientific Research, 1969), p. 205.

15. Allen B. Veaner, "Bibliographic Controls," in *Microform Utilization: The Academic Library Environment* (Denver, Colo.: University of Denver, 1971), p. 69.

16. Francis F. Spreitzer, "Developments in Copying, Micrographics,

and Graphic Communications, 1972," *Library Resources and Technical Services* 17 (1973): 23-26.

17. Paula Dranov, *Microfilm: The Librarian's View, 1976-1977* (White Plains, N.Y.: Knowledge Industry Publications, Inc., 1976), p. 31.

18. Montagnes, "Microfiche," p. 80.

19. Ibid., p. 81.

20. Frances G. Spigai, *The Invisible Medium: The State of the Art of Microform and a Guide to the Literature* (Stanford, Calif.: ERIC Clearinghouse on Media and Technology, 1973), p. 26.

21. Dranov, *Microfilm*, p. 69.

22. Jack Magarell, "A Publication Form That Has the Potential of Eliminating the Illustrated Book," *Chronicle of Higher Education* (May 10, 1976): 13.

23. Montagnes, "Microfiche," p. 70.

24. Interview with Ian Montagnes, May 15, 1977.

25. Montagnes, "Microfiche," p. 74.

26. University of Chicago Press promotion pamphlet entitled *Scholarly Publishing*.

27. Interview with Norman Mangouni, May 10, 1977.

28. Montagnes, "Microfiche," p. 83.

29. Interview with Norman Mangouni, May 10, 1977.

30. In 1973, Microtext Library Services, Clifton, New Jersey, was the first publisher to utilize this format.

31. Interview with Morris Phillipson, May 5, 1977.

32. University of Chicago Press pamphlet entitled *Text/Fiche: A New Publication Form*, p. 2.

33. *Text/Fiche: A New Publication Form*, p. 2.

34. *Guide to the Preparation of Text/Fiche* (Chicago: no date), prepared by the University of Chicago Press, p. 12.

35. Ibid.

36. Ibid., p. 13.

37. *Publishers Weekly*, "Chicago Press Launches New Micropublishing Project: Text/Fiche," (May 24, 1976): 41.

38. Ibid., p. 40.

39. Ibid., p. 41.

40. Ibid.

41. Caroline Kent, A review of "A Collection in the Making," *Art Library Society North American Newsletter* (January 1977): 31-32.

42. Magarell, "A Publication Form," p. 13.

43. *Saturday Review*, "Artsletter" (May 28, 1976): 41.

44. *Publishers Weekly*, "Chicago Press," p. 42.

45. Interview with Morris Phillipson, May 5, 1977.

9

CONCLUSIONS AND OBSERVATIONS

In less than fifty years, scholarly micropublishing has evolved from an idea to a thriving international business that serves the collections of every research library in the world. In the United States, library microform holdings have expanded dramatically. At the University of Illinois at Urbana alone, they increased forty-fold between 1961 and 1976, from 34,949 to 1,263,515. During the same period, the number of processed volumes and pamphlets grew from 3,272,412 to 5,368,666.[1]

In commercial terms, however, the industry's $70 million in annual sales do not approach the $550 million business the records management end of the micropublishing industry has become.[2] Furthermore, while micropublishing has vastly increased the accessibility of information vital to scholars throughout the world, it has not led to the far-reaching changes in either scholarship or library management which the industry's pioneers so optimistically predicted. Today, the once credible notion that microforms would eventually supplant books or reduce entire libraries to the size of a shoebox full of microfiche can be dismissed as the naive and impractical imaginings of overenthusiastic pioneers. While the significance of micropublishing's impact upon libraries and scholarship cannot be denied, it has conspicuously failed to fulfill some real and serious needs of both researchers and librarians.

What factors combined to produce this failure? Certainly, the advantages of microforms enumerated by their developers are as valid today as they were in the 1930s. They are (1) lightweight; (2) compact; (3) portable; (4) inexpensive and easy to duplicate; (5) convenient to store; (6) suitable for preservation of decaying original documents; (7) convertible to paper; and (8) easy to replace. Added to these assets is a new one that micropublishing pioneers never could have predicted: they lend themselves to rapid updating in combination with a computer.[3]

Ironically, today's much newer computer technology is fulfilling many of the scholarly and library management needs for which microforms once were seen as the ideal solution. With its speed, storage capacity, flexibility, and technological dependability, the computer offers libraries and scholars alike a powerful tool to meet a multitude of specialized needs. The eager acceptance of the computer in both the library and the scholarly communities is a marked contrast to the grudging reception accorded microforms. Indeed, the contrast between the success of the computer and the more limited impact of microforms illuminates many of the errors that prevented microforms from fulfilling their potential. The most striking of these errors are the means by which these two technologies were introduced, designed, and promoted. As one prominent librarian has noted, the promoters of microforms were, for the most part, librarians with little experience in marketing who mistakenly relied upon "the seemingly obvious logic of the microform idea to be readily understood and appreciated by and conveyed to others."[4] The computer industry had no such illusions. Its products and services were designed and promoted with user requirements in mind. As a new and powerful technology, computers had enormous appeal; nevertheless, their marketing was carefully tailored to the specialized needs of each type of potential user.

Other factors combined to limit microform potential in the years since the pioneering 1930s. Certainly, the intervention of World War II was detrimental to the development of the infant scholarly micropublishing industry, and more lucrative commercial usage after the war diverted valuable resources and innovative initiatives from scholarly micropublishing. Then, too, problems all but overlooked in the pioneering days have had a major impact on the growth of scholarly micropublishing and to a great extent have restricted its potential. As librarians and scholars became more familiar with micropublishing, they learned that there was more to it than snapping pictures and loading film into a viewer. The need for technical standards was soon apparent:

> Untrained, ill-informed or careless camera and machine operators turned out roll after roll of film that was over-exposed, underexposed, overdeveloped, underdeveloped, not properly fixed or washed out, out of focus, incomplete or otherwise defective. All too often the long-awaited microfilm was illegible or unsuitable for the intended use.[5]

Equipment also presented problems. Between 1936 and 1940, the only camera of professional quality and dependability was the Eastman Kodak Company's Recordak, a device which in the intervening forty years has undergone only slight modifications and is still in production. As far as reading machines were concerned, problems were rampant. Loading methods often were so complicated and confusing that even librarians and experienced researchers ended up with upside down or backwards film that sometimes would neither wind nor unwind. Worse, some loading errors damaged film. Microfiche equipment was hard to focus, and viewers for micro-opaque materials often offered hard-to-read low-contrast and illumination levels.

For librarians, a decision to purchase micropublications involved considerations far more numerous and complex than decisions to purchase books. Film quality, bibliographic control, the quality of the original material, storage conditions, and ease of access to specific documents had to be investigated. Most galling of all was the question of bibliographic control. Quite naturally, library patrons seeking information first consult the card catalog. Unfortunately, most large micropublishing products were not cataloged. Instead, the bibliographic controls, where they existed at all, were found in printed catalogs. But how were library patrons to know of the existence of these catalogs and the holdings they represented? It is not difficult to understand why all too often micropublications remained unused. The publishers themselves were reluctant to supply the bibliographic finding aids in the form of catalog cards; such undertakings would add too much to their costs. Less easy to understand is why libraries continued to acquire large micropublishing projects when access to them was frequently limited.

From another point of view, even the cost savings which microforms could offer libraries presented problems. True, materials could be more economically acquired, but the equipment for reading and copying these materials was an expense beyond the reach of many library budgets. Costs also precluded using microforms to fulfill some of the needs for which they were intended. Microphotography services required labor, preparation of bibliographic finding aids, and, eventually, adherence to technical standards if the end product was to be of any value. How then could libraries provide microcopies of their holdings free of charge as so many expected they would? Clearly, in their enthusiasm for microforms, many in the library community failed to take into account the practical realities of usage.

Eventually, one of the most saleable features of microforms was undermined as improved travel and communications reduced the need for micropublishing to duplicate materials in inconvenient places. Scholars the world over are now in much closer communication than could have been imagined in the 1930s.

In some ways, much has changed. In others, little is different: unquestionably, the book remains the most compatible medium for reading and research. The fears of scholars that microforms would eventually render books obsolete—as so many microform enthusiasts entranced with the potential of the medium once confidently predicted—have proved groundless. Emphasizing this point, Ian Montagnes of the University of Toronto Press, succinctly notes that "the book will survive. Even if the romance and detective novel succumb to the microscreen, the printed page will still be needed for works of contemplative reading and rereading."[6] However, microforms do continue to insure against the day when the economics of scholarly book publishing prohibit ready publication of monographs. Looking toward the future, Montagnes anticipated the role of microforms in scholarly publishing:

The microfiche will also stay with us. In the immediate future, this new ally in the dissemination of knowledge can help ensure that no worthy book need go out of print, no manuscript of merit rest unpublished for want of a large enough market, no documentation or illustration be omitted for lack of dollars. As the economic crunch gets tighter—as it becomes less and less possible to publish books that are over 300 pages or will not sell 1500, or 2500, or 3000 copies—microfiche may look more and more attractive, to publisher, author and reader.[7]

Rising production costs as well as increasing familiarity with microforms will, to a large extent, determine the future of scholarly micropublishing. Replacement of library card catalogs with computer output microform (COM) catalogs will undoubtedly accelerate their acceptance. Then, too, users will be affected by COM in its reference book applications and by the "hybrid" publications that combine books with microfiche illustrations.

Microforms will play a role—one that has not yet been determined—as a nationwide bibliographic network evolves. The extent of that role depends on how carefully needs are analyzed and microform services devised. Indeed, the question the industry faces today is not how efficiently it can produce micropublications, but how readily users will accept and appreciate the format as economics force the publication of more and more research materials in microform. Their ultimate usefulness depends on how conveniently micropublications can be read. If researchers continue to encounter difficulties with locating information, loading cumbersome reading equipment, finding what they want on a microfiche, and coping with fuzzy images, resistance to microform usage can hardly be expected to soften. The orverriding need now is for a microform system "geared to the characteristics of human beings and not the other way around."[8]

The fact that such a system does not yet exist speaks most eloquently of all to the ultimate failure of micropublishing to achieve the miracles its founding fathers predicted. In essence, their most grievous misconception was to attempt to impose technology on users, not as has so successfully been demonstrated by the computer industry, to select a goal and then shape the technology accordingly.

I cannot help but wonder how Robert C. Binkley would react to micropublishing today. He would most certainly be pleased that so many large collections are now available to scholars throughout the world. No doubt he would also be amazed that commercial, not nonprofit (or foundation-supported), ventures have been responsible for the growth of micropublishing in this country. Nevertheless, he would surely be disappointed that micropublishing has fallen so far short of what he saw as its potential. In the 1930s, it was possible to believe that one day books and libraries, too, would be replaced by compact and relatively inexpensive microforms. Unhappily, Binkley and the other pioneers ignored the human factors that should have been considered as micropublishing began to develop. For the most part, these men did not experience at first hand many of the difficulties that were to frustrate librarians and scholars. Most were administrators who did not have to rely on microforms on a daily basis in their own work. If they had, or if they had taken the time to analyze the study and work habits of the intended users, they might have understood and attempted at the outset to better serve their needs. As it was, the excitement the new technology generated in those days overshadowed the problems inherent in placing a machine between the human eye and the written word. As a result, the acknowledged benefits microforms conferred by making so much research material accessible to scholars have never been fully appreciated. Moreover, the legacy of resistance engendered by cumbersome reading machines with optical systems less than kind to the eyes has not been dissipated even by vast improvements in reading equipment.

Micropublishing can never completely overcome the inherent limitations of the medium, although better designed equipment may reduce many of the inconveniences its use presents. Still, it has served libraries and scholars well in the nearly fifty years since its inception. Quite clearly microforms will never be equated with books. Instead, they offer unique capabilities for presenting certain types of information.

Technical improvements yet to be devised should eventually overcome the usage problems that have proven so frustrating over the years. At this stage in micropublishing's development, it is apparent that microforms remain a practical means of fulfilling continuing needs. By appreciating them for what they are and ceasing to denigrate them for what they are not and never can be, the scholarly world can help insure an appropriate and successful role for micropublishing as it evolves from youth to vital maturity.

NOTES

1. Paul A. Napier, "Developments in Copying, Micrographics, and Graphic Communications, 1976," *Library Resources and Technical Services* 21 (1977): 210. There are ninety-four colleges and universities in North America that have microform holdings of at least 275,000 units (fiches, cards, reels, or opaques).

2. This figure was cited by the Resource Center of the National Micrographics Association, Silver Spring, Maryland, March 7, 1979.

3. Allen B. Veaner, "Micrographics: An Eventful Forty Years—What Next?," in *American Library Association Yearbook 1976* (Chicago: American Library Association, 1976), p. 49. Many of the ideas in this chapter are a result of the ideas expressed in this article.

4. Veaner, "Micrographics," p. 49.

5. Ibid., p. 52.

6. Ian Montagnes, "Microfiche and the Scholarly Publisher," *Scholarly Publishing* 5 (1975): 83.

7. Ibid.

8. Veaner, "Micrographics," p. 53.

GLOSSARY

This glossary defines essential terms used throughout this study. Definitions are necessarily abbreviated. Readers seeking a more extensive listing of micrographics terminology should consult *The Glossary of Micrographics* (Silver Spring, Md.: National Micrographics Association, 1973).

Archival quality. The ability of an entire processed microform to retain its original characteristics and to resist deterioration over time.

Camera-original microform. The microform that comes out of the camera, as opposed to the microform created by duplication.

Cartridge. A plastic single-core container for 16 mm or 35 mm microfilm. When mounted on an appropriate reader, microfilm from the cartridge is automatically threaded onto a take-up spool built into the reader.

Cassette. A plastic double-core container for 16 mm microfilm which encloses both a supply and take-up spool in a single housing.

Computer output microfilm. The end product of a process that converts machine-readable, computer-processable digital data to human-readable textual or graphic information on microfilm or microfiche without first creating paper documents.

Contrast. An expression of the relationship between high- and low-density areas of a photographic image or screen display.

COSATI. Acronym for the Committee on Scientific and Technical Information, used to denote a microfiche format consisting of sixty images reduced 18× and arranged in five rows and twelve columns.

Diazo process. Method of microform duplication in which film employing an emulsion of diazonium salts is exposed to ultraviolet light transmitted through a master microform. Salts are dispersed in areas of the microfilm corresponding to light areas of the original micro-image, while dark areas remain unaffected, forming a latent image that is developed with ammonia fumes.

Duplicate microforms. A microform created by duplicating an existing microform.

Duplicating microfilms. Microfilms designed for the creation of duplicate microforms rather than for use in cameras.

Enlarger/printer. A device designed for the automatic, high-speed, single- or multiple-copy production of enlarged prints from micro-images.

Eye-legible images. Images on microfilm that are large enough to be read by the unaided eye. Eye-legible images are generally employed in the first few target frames on microfilm or in the title row on microfiche, and serve to identify the microform and indicate its content.

Flat microforms. A grouping of microforms by physical shape. The flat microforms include microfiche, microfilm jackets, aperture cards, ultrafiche, and micro-opaques.

Generation. A measure of the remoteness of a particular microform from the original source document or computer output. The camera-original microform is a first-generation microform, a duplicate microform made from it is a second-generation microform, and so on.

Magnification. A measure of the size of a given linear dimension of a displayed micro-image compared to the size of the corresponding linear dimension of the micro-image itself. Magnification is expressed as 24×, 42×, 48×, and so on, where the displayed micro-image is enlarged twenty-four, forty-two, or forty-eight times.

Magnification ratio. Magnification expressed as a ratio—1:24, 1:42, 1:48, and so on.

Microcard. An opaque microform, 3 by 5 inches in size, on which micro-images are affixed in rows and columns. The reverse side of the card may contain additional micro-images or eye-legible bibliographic data.

Microfiche. A sheet of microfilm containing multiple micro-images in a two-dimensional grip pattern of rows and columns. The term is both singular and plural.

Microfilm. As a noun denotes fine-grain, high resolution film containing, or capable of containing, images greatly reduced in size. As a verb denotes the recording of micro-images on film.

Microform. A generic term for any information communication or storage medium containing images too small to be read without magnification.

Micrographics. A general term used to denote all activities relating to the creation or use of microforms.

Micro-image. Image too small to be read without magnification.

Micro-opaque. A microform distinguished by a paper rather than a film image support.

Microprint. Trade name for opaque microform created by the Readex Microprint Corporation. Unlike other microforms, Microprint is created by printing reduced document images on rag content card stock.

Micropublishing. The production of information in microform in place of, or prior to, its publication in paper form.

Micropublishing, original. The publication of information in microform in place of, or prior to, its publication in paper form.

Micropublishing, retrospective. The republication in multiple-copy microform of material previously published in paper form.

Micropublishing, simultaneous. The issuing of micropublication at the same time as paper form publication of the same material.

Polarity. The change or retention of the dark-to-light relationship of corresponding areas of a micro-image and the original source document or COM-generated display from which the micro-image was made.

Processing. The series of mechanical and chemical operations required to make latent micro-images visible.

Reader. A projection device that magnifies micro-images so they can be read with the unaided eye.

Reader/printer. A projection device that both magnifies micro-images for screen display and prints paper enlargements of displayed images on user demand.

Reduction. A measure of the number of times a given linear dimension of a document is reduced through microfilming. Reduction is expressed as 14×, 24×, 42×, and so on, where the reduced linear dimension is 1/14, 1/24, or 1/42 the length of its full-size counterpart.

Reduction ratio. The expression of reduction as a ratio—14:1, 24:1, 42:1, and so on.

Reel. A plastic or metal flanged holder for wound microfilm in 16 mm and 35 mm widths.

Resolution. As applied to microfilms and display devices, a measure of the ability of optical systems and photographic materials to render fine detail visible. Resolution is typically expressed as the number of lines per millimeter discernible in a micro-image and is determined by examining a microfilmed test target consisting of closely spaced lines of progressively decreasing size.

Roll microform. A generic term that encompasses microfilm on reels, in cartridges, and in cassettes.

Silver halide process. The dominant microfilming technology in which film coated with a light-sensitive emulsion of silver halide crystals suspended in gelatin is exposed to light reflected from a source document or generated by COM recorders. When exposed to light, silver halide crystals are converted to silver nuclei in areas of the film corresponding to light areas of the original. These altered crystals are converted to black silver grains during development.

Ultrafiche. Microfiche created at reduction in excess of 90×. In library applications, the term is often loosely used to denote fiche created at reductions in excess of 55×.

Vesicular process. Method of microform duplication in which film employing a light-sensitive emulsion suspended in a thermoplastic resin is exposed to ultraviolet light which creates pressure pockets that deform the emulsion, creating a latent image that is developed through heat.

Viewer. A hand-held magnifier that operates with an ambient or battery-powered light source.

Xerographic process. A method of micro-image enlargement which employs electrostatic charges to create a latent image on a charged intermediate surface and subsequently transfer the image to an oppositely charged sheet of ordinary paper. The process is employed in reader/printers and enlarger/printers.

BIBLIOGRAPHY

BOOKS

Ardern, L. L. *John Benjamin Dancer*. London: The Library Association, 1960.

Bahr, Alice H. *Microforms: The Librarian's View, 1978–1979*. White Plains, N.Y.: Knowledge Industry Publications, 1978.

Binkley, Robert C. *Manual on Methods of Reproducing Research Materials: A Survey Made for the Joint Committee on Materials for Research of the Social Science Research Council and the American Council of Learned Societies*. Ann Arbor, Mich.: Edwards Brothers, 1936.

———. *Methods of Reproducing Research Materials: A Survey Made for the Joint Committee on Materials for Research of the Social Science Research Council and the American Council of Learned Societies*. Ann Arbor, Mich.: Edwards Brothers, 1931.

Carleton, Ardis., ed. *Guide to Microforms in Print 1980*. Westport, Conn.: Microform Review, Inc., 1980.

Congressional Information Service. *User Guide*. Washington, D.C.: Congressional Information Service, 1975.

———. *The Working Papers of Congress*. Washington, D.C.: Congressional Information Service, 1975.

Council on Library Resources, Inc. *20th Annual Report of the Council on Library Resources, Inc*. Washington, D.C.: Council on Library Resources, Inc., 1976.

Dagron, Rene Patrice. *La Poste par Pigeons Voyageurs*. Tours: Typographie Lahure, 1871.

Dodson, Suzanne Cates., comp. *Microform Research Collections: A Guide*. Westport, Conn.: Microform Review, Inc., 1978.

Dranov, Paula. *Microfilm: The Librarian's View, 1976–1977*. White Plains, N.Y.: Knowledge Industry Publications, 1976.

Fisch, Max H., ed. *Selected Papers of Robert C. Binkley.* Cambridge, Mass.: Harvard University Press, 1948.

Fussler, Herman H. *Photographic Reproduction for Libraries: A Study of Administrative Problems.* Chicago: University of Chicago Press, 1942.

Gersheim, Helmut, and Gersheim, Alison. *The History of Photography.* New York: Oxford University Press, 1955.

Goldschmidt, Robert, and Otlet, Paul M. *Sur une Forme Nouvelle du Livre: Le Livre Microphtographique.* Brussels: Institut International de Bibliographie, 1906.

Hawken, William R. *Copying Methods Manual.* Chicago: American Library Association, 1966.

Hays, David G. *A Billion Books for Education in America and the World: A Proposal.* Santa Monica, Calif.: Rand Corp., 1968.

Leisinger, Albert H. *Microphotography for Archives.* Washington, D.C.: International Council on Archives, 1968.

Luther, Frederic. *Microfilm: A History, 1839–1900.* Silver Spring, Md.: National Microfilm Association, 1959.

Mann, James. *Reducing Made Easy.* Durham, N.C.: Moore Publishing Co., 1976.

Microform Market Place, 1980–1981. Westport, Conn.: Microform Review, Inc., 1980.

Morrison, Alta Bradley, comp. *Microform Utilization: The Academic Library Environment.* Denver, Colo.: University of Denver, 1971.

Nemeyer, Carol. *Scholarly Reprint Publishing in the United States.* New York: R. R. Bowker Co., 1971.

Raney, M. Llewellyn. *Microphotography for Libraries.* Chicago, Ill.: American Library Association, 1936.

Reno, Edward A. *League of Nations Documents, 1919–1946, a Descriptive Guide and Key to the Microfilm Collection.* New Haven, Conn.: Research Publications, 1973.

Rider, ·Fremont. *And Master of None.* Middletown, Conn.: Godfrey Memorial Library, 1955.

———. *The Scholar and the Future of the Research Library.* New York: Hadham Press, 1944.

Saffady, William. *Micrographics.* Littleton, Colo.: Libraries Unlimited, 1978.

Sibley, Elbridge. *Social Science Research Council, the First Fifty Years.* New York: Social Science Research Council, 1974.

Spigai, Frances G. *The Invisible Medium: The State of the Art of Microform and a Guide to the Literature.* Stanford, Calif.: ERIC Clearinghouse on Media and Technology, 1973.

Stevens, G.W.W. *Microphotography*. New York: John Wiley & Sons, 1968.

Librarians. Chicago: American Library Association, 1971.

———, ed. *Studies in Micropublishing*. Westport, Conn.: Microform Review, Inc., 1977.

Williams, Bernard J.S. *Miniaturised Communications: A Review of Microforms*. London: The Library Association, 1970.

Wooster, Harold. *Microfiche 1969—A User Survey*. Washington, D.C.: U.S. Air Force Office of Scientific Research, 1969.

ARTICLES

Adler, James B. "Indexing as the Key to Micropublishing: The Case History of the Congressional Information Service." *The Journal of Micrographics* (July 1971): 240.

"Artsletter." *Saturday Review* (May 28, 1976): 41.

Ballou, Hubbard W. "Photography and the Library." *Library Trends* (October 1956): 265-93.

Barnett, Claribel. "The Bibliofilm Service." *The Camera* (May 1935): 327-28.

Bechanan, H. Gordon. "Organization of Microforms in the Library." *Library Trends* (January 1960): 391-406.

Bendikson, L. "Dagron's Airgraph Postal Service of 1870." *Journal of Documentary Reproduction* (December 1941): 239-41.

Bennett, Ralph D. "Sheet Microfilm." *Journal of Documentary Reproduction* (March 1940): 39.

Binkley, Robert C. "New Tools for Men of Letters." *Yale Review* (November 1935): 520-37.

Born, Lester S. "History of Microform Activity." *Library Trends* (January 1960): 348-58.

Bradford, S. C. "Documentary Photography and Research." *Nature* (March 11, 1939): 393-95.

Butler, Brett. "Updating the Reference Book Through Microform Supplements." *Microform Review* 3 (1974): 27-32.

"Chicago Press Launches New Micropublishing Project: Text/Fiche." *Publishers Weekly* (May 24, 1976): 41.

Clapp, Verner W., and Jordan, Ralph T. "Re-evaluation of Microfilm as a Method of Book Storage." *College & Research Libraries* (January 1963): 5-15.

Dessauer, John. "Library Acquisitions: A Look into the Future." *Publishers Weekly* (June 16, 1975): 55.

Dickinson, R. R. "The Scholar and the Future of Microfilm." *American Documentation* (October 1966): 78–79.

Eckhardt, Caroline D., and Smith, John B. "Facts of Scholarly Micropublishing: Book-Length Works on Literature." *Publications of the Modern Language Association* 89 (1974): 366.

Eckles, R. B. "Some Problems in Scholarly Uses of Microphoto Publication." *American Archivist* (October 1964): 565–67.

Ewer, D. W. "A Biologist's Reflections on Libraries and Library Service." *South African Libraries* (October 1961): 53–56, 74.

Fessenden, Reginald A. "Use of Photography in Data Collections." *Electrical World* (August 22, 1896): 224.

Fussler, Herman H. "Microfilm and Libraries." In William Madison Randall, ed. *Acquisition and Cataloging of Books.* Chicago: University of Chicago Press, 1940, p. 346.

———. "Photographic Reproduction of Research Materials." *Library Trends* (April 1954): 532–44.

Grieder, Elmer M. "Ultrafiche Libraries: A Librarian's View." *Microform Review* (January 1972): 85–100.

"Harvard Project for Microfilming Newspapers." *Journal of Documentary Reproduction* (March 1939): 41–43.

Hawken, William R. "Microform Standardization: The Problem of Research Materials and a Proposed Solution." *Journal of Micrographics* (January 1968): 14–27.

———. "Systems Instead of Standards." *Library Journal* (September 15, 1973): 2515–25.

Henry, E. A. "Books on Film: Their Use and Care." *Library Journal* (March 15, 1932): 215–17.

Herschel, J.F.W. "New Photographic Process." *Athenaeum* (July 9, 1853): 831.

Hickey, Mary E. "Inter Documentation Company: A History." *Microform Review* 3 (1974): 107–12.

Holmes, Donald C. "Electrostatic Photoreproduction at the United States Library of Congress." *UNESCO Library Bulletin* 18 (1961): 6.

Jeffrey, Thomas E. "The Papers of Benjamin Latrobe: New Approaches to the Micropublication of Historical Records." *Microform Review* 6 (1977): 82–86.

Johnson, Amandus. "Some Early Experiences in Microphotography." *Journal of Documentary Reproduction* (January 1938): 9–19.

Johnson, R. P. "The Use of 35-Millimeter Camera in European Libraries. *Library Journal* 60 (April 1, 1935): 294.

Jordan, Robert T. "The 'Complete Package' College Library." *College & Research Libraries* (September 1962): 405–409.

Kent, Caroline. A review of "A Collection in the Making." *Art Library Society North American Newsletter* (January 1977): 31–32.

Kerr, Chester. "What to Publish at Yale." *Scholarly Publishing* (October 1974): 216.

Laflin, Marjorie A. "Micropublishing Potential in Professional Journal Publications." *Journal of Micrographics* 10 (1977): 279–83.

LaHood, Charles G., Jr. "Production and Uses of Microfilm in the Library of Congress Photoduplication Service." *Special Libraries* (February 1960): 68–71.

Luther, Frederic. "Earliest Experiments in Microphotography." *American Documentation* (August 1951): 167–70.

Magarell, Jack. "A Publication Form That Has the Potential of Eliminating the Illustrated Book." *Chronicle of Higher Education* (May 10, 1976): 13.

Mangouni, Norman. "Micropublishing Among the University Presses." *Microform Review* (October 1974): 251.

Massey, D. W. "Aching Eye: The Use of Microforms and Viewers by Scholars and Researchers." *Virginia Librarian* (Winter 1970): 22–24.

McDonald, J. "Case Against Reading Microfilm." *American Archivist* (October 1975): 345–56.

Meckler, Alan M. "Smaller and Smaller." *Times Literary Supplement* (September 22, 1978): 1061.

"Mene, Mene." *Saturday Review* (November 20, 1937): 8.

Montagnes, Ian. "Microfiche and the Scholarly Publisher." *Scholarly Publishing* (October 1975): 63–84.

Morehead, Joe. "Review of CIS Index." *Reference Quarterly* (Winter 1970): 158–60.

Napier, Paul A., Steiner, Annette D., and Woodward, Rupert C. "The Library Resources Inc., *Library of American Civilization* Demonstration at the George Washington University Library." *Microform Review* (July 1974): 153–57.

Page, B. S., Sayce, L. S., and Patterson, E. F. "Microphotography: Standards in Format, Storage, and Cataloguing." *The Library Association Record* 40 (1938): 212–16.

Pike, Nicholas. "The Micrograph." *Photographic News* 9 (1864): 21.

Power, Eugene. "Microfilm in Europe, 1939." *Journal of Documentary Reproduction* (March 1939): 254.

———. "O-P Books: A Library Breakthrough." *American Documentation* (October 1958): 273–76.

———. "Report on Progress on Filming English Books Before Before 1550." *Journal of Documentary Reproduction* (January 1938): 45.

———. "University Microfilms." *Journal of Documentary Reproduction* (March 1939): 21.

Puckette, C. M. "Current New York Times Available on Film." *Journal of Documentary Reproduction* (March 1939): 38-39.

Reynolds, Catharine J. "League of Nations Documents and Serial Publications, 1919-1946 Review Article." *Microform Review* (October 1973): 272-73.

Rider, Fremont. "The Future of the Research Library." *College & Research Libraries* (September 1944): 301-308.

Riggs, John A. "The State of Microtext Publications." *Library Trends* 8 (1960): 372-79.

Salmon, Stephen. "User Resistance to Microforms in the Research Library." *Microform Review* 3 (1974): 103-109.

Seidell, Atherton. "Cost of Microfilm Copying in Libraries." *Journal of Documentary Reproduction* (September 1941): 164-67.

———. "Place of Microfilm Copying in Library Organizations." *Science* (August 1, 1941): 114-15.

Sidebotham, Joseph. "On Micro-photography." *Photographic Journal* 6 (1857): 91.

Spreitzer, Francis F. "Developments in Copying, Micrographics and Graphic Communications, 1971." *Library Resources and Technical Services* 15 (1972): 135-54.

———. "Developments in Copying, Micrographics, and Graphic Communications, 1972." *Library Resources and Technical Services* (Spring 1973): 23-26.

Stevens, Rolland E. "Microform Revolution." *Library Trends* (January 1971): 379-95.

Tate, Vernon D. "From Binkley to Bush." *American Archivist* (July 1947): 249-57.

———. "Microphotography in Wartime." *Journal of Documentary Reproduction* (March 1942): 129.

———. "Reflex and Photocopying." In *The Complete Photographer*. New York: National Education Alliance, 1942.

Taylor, Robert S. "Libraries and Micropublication." *Microform Review* (January 1972): 25-27.

Tennant, John. "Readex Microprints." *Journal of Documentary Reproduction* (March 1940): 69.

Veaner, Allen B. "Bibliographic Controls." In *Microform Utilization: The Academic Library Environment*. Denver, Colo.: University of Denver, 1971, p. 69.

———. "Micrographics: An Eventful Forty Years—What Next?" In

American Library Association Yearbook 1976. Chicago: American Library Association, 1976, pp. 45-56.

Weber, David. "The Foreign Newspaper Microfilm Project." *Harvard Library Bulletin* (Spring 1956): 275-81.

Weis, M. M. "Case for Microfilming." *American Archivist* (January 1959): 15-24.

Welter, Rush. "The Publication of Books with Small Potential Sale, and Related Problems." In *Problems of Scholarly Publication of the American Council of Learned Societies*. New York: American Council of Learned Societies, 1959, pp. 28-35.

Willemse, John. "The Future of Microfiche in Libraries: Possibilities for Better Service." *South African Librarian* (July 1969), pp. 32-39.

PAMPHLETS

American Council of Learned Societies, *A Summary Statement of Its Work and Its Plans for a Fiftieth Anniversary Capital Development Program*, 1969.

Gatzke, Hans W. "Introduction," in pamphlet, *League of Nations Documents and Serial Publications, 1919-1946*. New Haven, Conn.: Research Publications, Inc. Not dated.

Guide to the Preparation of Text/Fiche. Pamphlet prepared by the University of Chicago Press. Not dated.

The Library of American Civilization. Pamphlet prepared by Library Resources, Inc. Not dated.

Scholarly Publishing. Pamphlet published by the University of Chicago Press. Not dated.

Text/Fiche: A New Publication Form. Pamphlet published by the University of Chicago Press. Not dated.

CATALOGS

Carrollton Press catalog entitled *1978-79 Publications List*.

Congressional Information Service catalog entitled *CIS 1978-1979 Catalog*.

Greenwood Press catalog entitled *1978 Greenwood Microform Catalog*.

Kraus-Thomson Organization catalog entitled *General Catalog 1978-1979*.

Lost Cause Press catalog entitled *Lost Cause Press Microfiche Collections 1977-1978, Volume Five/Number One*.

Microfilming Corporation of America catalog entitled *1978 Publications*.

Micro Photo catalog entitled *1979–1980 Catalog.*

Research Publications catalog entitled *1979 Descriptive Catalogue of Microfilm Collections and Bibliographies.*

University Microfilms International catalog entitled *A Catalog of Research Materials.*

University Microfilms International catalog entitled *Serials in Microform 1979–1980.*

PAPERS

Papers of the American Council of Learned Societies. The Library of Congress. Washington, D.C.

The Archive of Micrographics. Annapolis, Md.

Papers of the Association of Research Libraries. Washington, D.C.

Hubbard W. Ballou Papers. New York, N.Y.

Alex Baptie Papers. Naples, Fla.

Albert Boni Papers. New York, N.Y.

Memorandum of Staff Director of Joint Committee on Printing to Senator Howard W. Cannon. Washington, D.C.

Papers of the Microfiche Foundation. Delft Technological University Library. Delft, Holland.

Rockefeller Foundation Papers. Tarrytown, N.Y.

UNPUBLISHED MANUSCRIPTS

Boehm, Eric H. "Current Emphasis in the Dissemination of Information about Manuscripts." Paper presented at the Conference on the Publication of American Historical Manuscripts, University of Iowa, March 13, 1975.

Luther, Frederic. Untitled manuscript.

McGowan, Frank M. "The Association of Research Libraries, 1932–1962." University of Pittsburgh, Ph.D. dissertation.

LETTERS

Letter from Dr. J. Goebel to Alan Meckler dated May 12, 1977.

Letter from Dr. J. Goebel to Alan Meckler dated May 23, 1977.

INTERVIEWS

Interview with James B. Adler, Washington, D.C., July 7, 1977.
Interview with Alex Baptie, Naples, Fla., November 17, 1976.
Interview with Albert Boni, Daytona Beach, Fla., November 16, 1976.
Interview with Wilf Deakin, London, England, June 2, 1977.
Interview with Henri deMink, Leiden, Holland, October 8, 1977.
Interview with Charles Farnsley, Washington, D.C., October 9, 1978.
Interview with Samuel Freedman, New Haven, Conn., August 12, 1976.
Interview with William Hawkins, Paris, France, February 20, 1977.
Interview with Irving Leonard, South Hadley, Mass., January 18, 1978.
Interview with Norman Mangouni, Albany, N.Y., May 10, 1977.
Interview with Keyes Metcalfe, Boston, Mass., May 5, 1978.
Interview with Morris Phillipson, Chicago, Ill., May 5, 1977.
Interview with Eugene Power, Ann Arbor, Mich., July 20, 1976.
Interview with Vernon Tate, Annapolis, Md., November 14, 1976.

Index

Filmograph, 21
Fiskoscope, 24
Foreign Newspaper Microfilm
    Project, 33-34
Fox-Talbot, William Henry, 4
Freedman, Samuel, 59-60, 65, 96,
    99, 102, 116
Fussler, Herman, 40n.54, 60

Gelatt, Charles, 55-56
Gersheim, Alison, 4
Gersheim, Helmut, 4
Glaisher, John, 6-7
Glueck, Leonard, 59
Goebel, Joseph, 35, 41n.69, 76
Goldschmidt, Robert, 11-14, 35
Government Printing Office,
    66-68. See also *Index to Con-
    gressional Documents and
    Microfiche Service*
Greenwood Press, vi, 91, 95n.10
Guide to Microfilming Practices, 68
Guide to Microforms in Print, 94

Handbuch der Heliographie, 9
Harvard University, 31, 33-34, 59
Hawkins, William, 76
Herschel, Sir John, 4, 6-7
Hessert, R. M., 16
Huntington Library, 25, 31

*Index to Congressional Documents
    and Microfiche Service*, 116-
    32. See also Congressional
    Information Service
*Index to Publications of the United
    States Congress*, 90
Inter Documentation Company,
    77
Interlibrary loan, 35, 41n.66

John Crear Library, 10
Johnson, Amandus, 13-15
Joint Committee on Materials for
    Research, 19, 23, 25-26, 43

*Journal of Documentary Repro-
    duction*, 32

Kraus-Thomson Organization,
    91-92

*League of Nations Documents
    Collection*, 96-114
Levin, Howard M., 149-51
Lewis, Lucy M., 35
Library of American Civilization,
    74, 84n.33
Library of Congress, 10, 34, 59,
    67
Library Resources, Inc., 74
Liveright, Horace, 51
Lost Cause Press, 92
Luther, Frederic, xii

McCarthy, George L., 15-16
Madsen, Soren C., 9
Mangouni, Norman, 135-36, 138,
    142
Metcalf, Keyes D., 33, 60
*Methods of Reproducing Research
    Materials*, 20
Microcard, 53-55
Microcard Corporation, 55-56,
    59, 65
Microcard Foundation, 56
Microfilm: A History, xii
Microfilm Norms, 68
Microfilming Corporation of
    America, 92-93
Microform Review, xii
Micro Photo Corporation, 59-60,
    93, 99
Microprint, 52-53, 54
Montagnes, Ian, 137, 139, 141,
    143, 157
Morrow, John H., 8

National Bureau of Standards, 68
National Historical Publications
    Commission, 78

About the Author

Alan Marshall Meckler received his doctorate from Columbia University; he is the publisher of *Microform Review*. He is the author of *The Draft and Its Enemies*.